The Art of Data Analysis

The Art of Data Analysis

Nontechnical Skills for Data Analysts

Alberto Scappini

Contents

Introduction

Verona (Italy), September 2004. I was about to start my first class at the university. The subject: Spanish literature. During high school, I was fascinated by humanistic studies such as history, arts, and literature. During my spare time, I was also trying to produce small "pieces of art." For example, I tried to start a novel about my young life, write poems remembering a past love, or do a painting applying the principles of perspective when we were studying Leon Battista Alberti. After three years, however, I started to look for new challenges and think more seriously about the job I wanted to do. Unfortunately, what I was studying was not leading me toward my goal, and I decided to change my country and my education. I went to Switzerland to study economics. My interest in economics, math, and statistics kept on increasing, to the point that even after completing university, I continued studying these subjects on Coursera and acquired a master's in BI and Big Data in Madrid, Spain. In the beginning, I regretted all the time I had "wasted" on humanistic studies. I was lagging behind other people who were competing for the jobs I wanted. I wished I had studied statistics and programming when I was younger. But then I realized that even if I had a lot to catch up in those skills, I had something that made me somehow different in a positive way. I had a better grasp of business problems, I was always thinking strategically, and I could easily and effectively present results. I finally understood that humanistic and "soft skills" studies helped me tremendously to be a better analyst. After this *epiphany*, I started to complement my continuous training in statistics and programming with training related to communication, creativity, public speaking, or design—aware that these skills make me a better analyst than I would have been without them.

It's a pity that the focus of data analysis is almost exclusively on statistics and programming. Yes, you may read that analysts need to know the business, be creative, communicate results well, and so forth, but these skills are typically viewed as "nice to have" skills. That's why I decided to write a book about the most insightful "soft" skills I've learned and that have proven to be very helpful in data analysis. I'm not pretending to reveal any new or extraordinary information. I'm only meaningfully organizing what I've learned from many authors far more expert than me in their respective domains—I sincerely thank them for their work. I encourage you not to stop at the content of this book but to investigate further through the resources I've used.

WHO IS THIS BOOK FOR?

This book is for all data analysts who want to learn or improve nontechnical skills to make a difference in their jobs. If you are a technically oriented analyst, this book will help you learn the fundamentals of nontechnical skills. If you are a business-oriented analyst, this book will help you consolidate your nontechnical skills and probably learn some new ones.

To illustrate the usefulness of this book, I'd like to use the famous Pareto rule, which states 20% of effort is needed to obtain the knowledge to solve 80% of problems (figure 1).

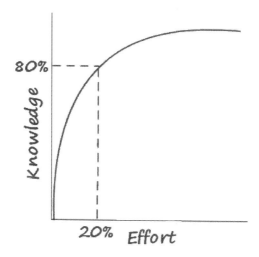

Figure 1: Pareto rule in the effort–knowledge relationship

This book is about the core 20% of nontechnical skills that represent the basic knowledge needed in 80% of the cases. If you are a data scientist, this book will help you achieve this 80%. If you are a business-oriented analyst, however, this only represents the basics and you will have to spend the other 80% of effort to get the extra 20% of knowledge in nontechnical skills to excel in them.

First, we explore the principles of creativity and how to use it in data analytics by adopting several techniques ("Be Creative"). Then we look at the importance of knowing your business, accompanied by a short overview of the main business concepts, as well as how to implement a sound data strategy aligned with your company's objectives ("Know the Business" and "Think Strategically"). In "Understand the Human Mind," I help you understand why humans seem to behave "irrationally" and how to use these concepts to improve data analysis. In the next chapter, "Go Beyond Statistics," I explain several "nontechnical" data analysis techniques, such as heuristics and analytics. Even if statistics is the backbone of data analysis, thanks to these techniques, the quality of your work can improve exponentially. Finally, the last part of the book is dedicated to communication-related skills. Since data analysts have to deal with both providers and other departments, they have to be good at negotiating ("Be a Negotiator"). Further, we look at the basic principles of communication and storytelling ("Be a Communicator") that will help you become a good writer, public speaker and designer ("Be a Writer," "Be a Public Speaker," "Be a Designer"). I will especially emphasize the content of the last chapter because the ability to create good data visualizations and dashboards is a major core competence of any analyst.

Be Creative

Problem-solving is the essence of what a data analyst has to do, and creativity is a fundamental ability to solve problems. Broadly speaking, creative thinking means exploring a problem in a different way and finding alternative solutions that solve it effectively. Several theories and techniques have been developed to help boost creativity, but almost all are based on two theories about how the brain works.

The first theory concerns the way our brain processes information. It is a machine programmed for the creation of patterns based on external information. Thanks to this network of patterns, the brain can identify a known person in a fraction of a second, can solve more complex problems using an analogy with similar situations, and can infer why something has happened because of the stored information about cause-effect relationships. When a new piece of information comes in, our patterns are altered, but there is a general tendency to filter or perceive information according to our principles (our deepest existing patterns). For example, a religious person would filter or alter new information that potentially undermines his or her beliefs. Since the brain prefers status quo over change, creativity can be a very difficult task since it means questioning assumptions and existing patterns.

The second theory concerns the different abilities that different parts of the brain have. Either it is logic versus intuition, verbal versus spatial, or the different "intelligences" (logic, mathematics, motion, interpersonal, etc.), creativity arises when different parts work together to reach a common conclusion.

According to Edward De Bono,[1] there is more than ever a need for creativity, and creative thinking will soon be extremely important in business divisions like finance or human resources. "Serious Creativity" can be the competitive advantage of a company in a world that is more and more commodified. If you link this to the fact that in recent years, data analytics has been considered to be the "ultimate" source of competitive advantage for companies, the combination of the two concepts can have

---

1 Edward De Bono, *Serious Creativity: Using the Power of Lateral Thinking to Create New Ideas* (New York: HarperCollins Publishers, 1993).

remarkable results. A data analyst must be able to combine these two concepts: be a logical analyst on one hand and also be creative on the other in order to create "magic." Simple data analysis cannot produce new concepts; it can only repeat old patterns. Instead, you should have the capacity to change radically the way you see things and you can reach this only though creativity.

To be creative, first gain confidence about your inner creativity and overcome the fears of the unknown, of being judged, and of taking the first step. Second, start producing the best stimuli (inputs) to nourish your creativity—for example, by learning from different and unrelated fields, talking to interesting people, or looking at the world with innocence and curiosity. Third, be effective, that is, focus on the important things and commit to them with perseverance. Finally, it is important to understand the process of creative thinking and try to reproduce it. I will conclude this section with some interesting creative techniques that you can use in data analysis.

Confidence

IDEO founder David Kelley and IDEO partner Tom Kelley[2] claim that we all are creative people but we have forgotten how to behave like them. When we grow up, our creativity gets inhibited due to social norms, conservative education, and various responsibilities. Often it is not the question of improving or learning how to be creative, but to rediscover our inner child, namely being confident in our ability to be creative. David and Tom Kelley demonstrate the example of Stanford professor and psychologist Albert Bandura who helped people to overcome the phobia of snakes using a series of increasingly demanding interactions with them. First, these people started by just watching snakes from afar, eventually approaching them, and finally touching them. A similar approach can be applied when you are facing the four fears that prevent you from being creative.

The first fear, "fear of the messy unknown," makes people stick to their own ideas. It is more comfortable to stay at your desk and do what you know, instead of standing up, talking to people, going outside the company, and taking the risk of hearing something you prefer not to hear. You have to take small steps and leave your comfort zone.

People usually prefer to stick to safe solutions since the opinion of other coworkers and bosses are much too important, and here comes the second fear: the "fear of being judged"—in case of failure or in case you propose anything that seems ridiculous. However, this blocks innovative ideas. The first step is to stop judging yourself. The second step is to systematically write down your ideas and force you to dedicate some time to them. You should also define ambitious goals concerning the number of ideas you write down in a certain period of time. Some of these ideas may not seem so ridiculous at a second glance.

Even if you finally embrace a creative idea, taking the first step is quite challenging. You can spend a lot of time planning but you should dare to

---

2   Tom Kelley and David Kelley, *Creative Confidence: Unleashing the Creative Potential Within Us All* (London: William Collins, 2015).

4

stop "getting ready and get started." Overcoming the third fear, fear of the first step, means to stop focusing on the overall problem, breaking it down into smaller, manageable pieces, and starting to face them one by one.

Confidence also means admitting that your idea might not be good and maybe the ideas of other people are better. When you work in a team or accept other people's ideas, you get over the fourth fear, the "fear of losing control," since you are ceding it.

Finally, remember that no idea is right or wrong, so don't dismiss any idea at the beginning and embrace missteps, which are a part of the creative process.

Stimuli

Your creative outputs will depend on the inputs that you are feeding your brain. Since the brain's capacity to absorb and interiorize inputs is limited, you have to focus on the most challenging, relevant, and diverse ones. A good practice is to define a plan of study and activities based on what you are curious about, what you will need, and what would be good for you.

Knowledge gained through study, training, and experience is fundamental for data analysts to better understand and tackle problems. Without expertise in a particular field, it is quite improbable to emerge with a proper solution; this is the way you should always try to nourish your knowledge. But don't just zero in on the knowledge concerning your field. Information from different fields can generate innovative solutions. Moreover, be aware that too much knowledge in a specific area is detrimental for creativity because it impedes you from going off the beaten path and makes it more difficult to accept new patterns for solving a problem. A data analyst needs to have solid business acumen that he or she can gain with experience and must have enough technical knowledge to conduct data analysis but not too much as to make him or her less creative. He or she must broaden his knowledge spectrum by studying disciplines not related to the business, by learning new technical skills, or by talking with professionals of different fields. It's important to also consider unlikely sources of stimuli and not to forget that the body needs to be in good shape and stimulated to foster creativity.

To be more open to external stimuli, behave like how you did as a child—observe everything with innocence and curiosity, without preconceptions or filters. Engage in unstructured activities and do them just for the joy of doing them. You can take your problem and move it to a different reality, for example in prison or to Mars. How would it look? How would you solve it in this new reality? [3]

---

3 R. Keith Sawyer, *Explaining Creativity: The Science of Human Innovation* (New York: Oxford University Press, 2013).

Another extremely important source of stimuli is talking to other people. Other people are an incredible source of inspiration for creativity since they help you see outside of yourself and your problems. You should create stimulating relationships by engaging with visionary people, possibly outside of your close circle and with different backgrounds. Don't be ashamed of imitating brilliant people. Do it, give credit if necessary, and one day you will find your personal voice. You can also leverage the idea generation potential of different people through teamwork. If you plan to do this, try to include different people in the group, as Tom and David Kelley have suggested:[4]

- The visionary who always knows which is the next step
- The problem finder who doesn't waste time and comes directly to the point
- The individualist who contradicts everybody
- The connector who keeps the group united
- The craftsman who is able to apply the ideas to the real world
- The technologist who is the nerd of the group and usually researches the connection between things
- The entrepreneur who converts ideas into businesses
- The multidisciplinary facilitator who is able to apply concepts from different disciplines breaking the barriers among them

---

4 Kelley and Kelley, *Creative Confidence*.

Effectiveness

Time and energy are limited resources and you have to spend them efficiently and effectively. Todd Henry, in his book *The Accidental Creative*,[5] suggests that in order to be effectively creative, you have to focus on things that really matter in a systematic way. This will allow you to find your "creative rhythm," which will allow you to be constantly creative. You first have to focus on important things and avoid distractions. These important things are those that deserve most of your energy and time, so plan your weekly, monthly, and quarterly commitments carefully.

Time too has to be managed wisely; however, try to obsess less on efficiency and focus instead on time-effectiveness. Sometimes it may seem that an activity is a waste of time, but if it is an important activity you should commit to it. Try to overcome the problem by questioning the assumptions, thinking about how you solved similar problems. A good practice to reduce waste of time (and reasoning energy) is to start the day with a ritual[6] (exercise, reading, etc.) and have a routine for less important activities. In an interview Barack Obama told *Vanity Fair* (October 2012),: "You'll see I wear only gray or blue suits. I'm trying to pare down decisions. I don't want to make decisions about what I'm eating or wearing. Because I have too many other decisions to make. You need to focus your decision-making energy. You need to routinize yourself. You can't be going through the day distracted by trivia."

Commitment is the key to be effective in generating creative solutions since creativity is usually not the result of a stroke of genius but a consequence of hard work and continuous practice. However, the creative outcome is too often simplistically related to the serendipitous magic moment (i.e., the "spark") but the hard work behind great discoveries is usually neglected. Take for example the story of Newton's apple. Besides the fact of its veracity, what we like to hear is the genius spark that created

5   Todd Henry, *The Accidental Creative: How to Be Brilliant at a Moment's Notice* (New York: Penguin, 2013).
6   Twyla Tharp and Mark Reiter, *The Creative Habit: Learn It and Use It for Life: A Practical Guide* (New York: Simon & Schuster, 2006).

magic. However, we ignore the years of study, preparation, experimentation, and failure without which the spark wouldn't have generated any idea. As Erik Wahl has said, "This is the first truth you have to understand about creative endeavors: the spark comes to life at the expense of the grind. You will always run into problems when your efforts stop at the initial spark because rarely is the first spark the hottest, most potent spark."[7]

Steven Pressfield[8] calls this "perseverance" which is fundamental to becoming a "pro" in creativity, after having fought resistance (namely the four fears mentioned before in this chapter). Pressfield specifies that one should focus on the process instead of the end or outcome. This is critical for data artists. Even if they have to define clear goals, they don't have to be attached to the outcome since it can be unclear or even unforeseeable. They should instead focus on the process and perseverate despite the difficulties.

---

7 Erik Wahl, *The Spark and the Grind: Ignite the Power of Disciplined Creativity* (New York: Portfolio/Penguin, 2017).
8 Steven Pressfield, *The War of Art: Winning the Inner Creative Battle* (New York: Rugged Land, 2002).

Process

The brain is a machine that always looks for patterns, thinks in terms of patterns, and transforms new information into patterns. These patterns are used to deal with situations both consciously and unconsciously. However, when you have to deal with new situations the brain cannot resort to stored patterns and this is when System 2 (the analytical one, as explained in the book *Thinking, Fast and Slow* by Daniel Kahneman)—the part of our brain that uses reasoning and logic—comes into play.

Creative ideas seem logical once interiorized since the new pattern has been formed and it is related to our previous patterns. However, this may mislead you and make you think that you can use logic to find out creative ideas. This is often not possible since new patterns seem logical only after "saving" them in our brain, but before you had to "cut across" your existing patterns and move to the less obvious ideas.

Edward De Bono[9] identifies four types of reasoning:

- Backward thinking: This process analyzes past or existing situations and works over them to explain effects.
- Forward thinking: This process is more concerned with bringing about an effect by using creativity, invention, and moving toward something new rather than looking at old patterns.
- Vertical thinking: This is a rational, sequential, and analytical approach toward problems. Logic is used in a series of sequential steps until reaching the "right" solution.
- Lateral thinking: This can be seen as the opposite of vertical thinking and it is based more on the internal process of information restructuring than the use of external information. While vertical thinking can be seen as digging a deeper hole, lateral thinking is digging the hole in a different place.

---

9 Edward De Bono, *Lateral Thinking: Creativity Step by Step* (New York: Perennial Library, 2015).

According to the author, all the types of thinking are fundamental for problem-solving; however, lateral thinking is the one that is able to make jumps and reach unordinary solutions to problems. With lateral thinking, you tackle them from different perspectives and eliminate the barriers that limit your reasoning (assumptions). Compared to vertical thinking, instead of analyzing critically and developing information, lateral thinking restructures it by changing or questioning the underlying assumptions. To quote Tom Goodwin, "Uber, the world's largest taxi company, owns no vehicles. Facebook, the world's most popular media owner, creates no content. Alibaba, the most valuable retailer, has no inventory. And Airbnb, the world's largest accommodation provider, owns no real estate. Something interesting is happening." All these companies revolutionized several sectors by questioning some basic assumptions about their businesses. Questioning basic assumptions means also asking different questions. Instead of asking "How can I make this product reach the most consumers?" try "What most consumers want me to produce to satisfy their needs?" This process not only generates new ideas thanks to new assumptions but also to the very fact of creating conflicts among assumptions. When two opposing assumptions are accepted and validated, this clash generates new ideas and solutions.[10] In fact, the "conflict" between apparently unrelated or even opposite elements can be leveraged extensively to create new ideas. It has been proven that when you work with different "intelligences" at the same time (linguistic, logical-mathematical, musical, bodily kinesthetic, spatial, interpersonal, and intrapersonal), you are more creative[11] since this forces your brain to create new connections and not just to stick to the old patterns.

Another problem with conventional thinking is oversimplification. When confronted with a complex situation (the majority of situations in real life), conventional thinkers tend to filter the features related to it, focusing on the most obvious aspects and leaving outside important elements. At

10 Robert Epstein, *Creativity Games for Trainers: A Handbook of Group Activities for Jumpstarting Workplace Creativity* (New York: Training McGraw-Hill, 1996).
11 Howard Gardner, *Intelligence Reframed: Multiple Intelligences for the 21st Century* (New York: Basic Books, 1999).

this point, with a poorer representation of reality, the conventional thinker applies simplified linear cause-effect relationships between elements, where x produces y. Finally, the resolution will be the result of a binary process between A and B. The solution will not be the optimal one, but the best trade-off between the pros and cons of A and B.

The integrative thinker,[12] instead, will embrace complexity and consider the situation with a broader view, taking into account less obvious features as well. This is not an easy task since it is necessary to cope with the feeling of fear that arises when you don't control the situation. In addition to this, the integrative thinker sees the elements of the situation as interconnected pieces that are viewed in the context of the whole. Relationships are multidirectional and nonlinear, as opposed to the linear relationship of the conventional way of thinking. The integrative thinkers don't try to find a solution using a binary process, but they can tackle the tension between opposing ideas thanks to which they create new innovative solutions that are neither A nor B, but may be C, D, or E.

Unlike the conventional thinker, the data artist prefers gathering varied experiences to broaden his or her toolkit instead of gathering experiences that reinforce the actual tools or skills. He or she is able to use an optimal balance of mastery (gained through experience) and originality (desire to experiment), like Leonardo da Vinci mixed art and science to produce masterpieces. To be an integrative thinker, the data artist can use three tools suggested by Roger Martin :

- Generative reasoning: Instead of using only deductive reasoning (reaching conclusions with logic, using a general rule, and applying it to the specific situation) and inductive reasoning (observing evidence and deriving a general conclusion that is probable, but not certain), the integrative thinker also uses abductive reasoning. Despite inductive reasoning, the abductive one is based on the

---

12 Roger L. Martin, *The Opposable Mind: Winning Through Integrative Thinking* (Boston, MA: Harvard Business Press, 2009).

observation of incomplete evidence. Possible solutions can only be reached through creative leaps, intuition, or imagination.

- Causal modeling: The inference of causal relationships to solve problems can be determined at different levels, from a basic linear relationship (x causes y), to a multidirectional set of relationships, or to a metaphorical tool where the problem is seen through a metaphor.
- Assertive inquiry: It means seeking new points of view and new models (including models that contradict your own model) in order to reach creative solutions.

You have to embrace complexity, but sometimes this can be overwhelming and instead of boosting creativity you get stacked. To avoid this, split the complex problem into small feasible ones, proceeding with several iterations until you reach the outcome. In addition to this, the very path to creativity is neither linear nor like a "bolt of lightning that lit up the world in a single, brilliant flash." Instead, it is a continuous process comprised of "tiny steps, bits of insight, and incremental changes."[13] You have to follow and exploit these "zig zags" instead of fighting them, and you will reach creativity.

Finally, "vision without execution is hallucination."[14] Ideas per se don't have any value; you must make them a reality. The ability to implement ideas is as important as the ability to generate ideas. To improve the ability to implement ideas, you must properly balance two processes: the unstructured open generation of ideas and the critical evaluation of ideas. Without the right balance between creative thinking and critical thinking, you either risk generating many unfeasible ideas or generating just a few conventional ideas. The first step for implementation is to start visualizing your ideas. For example, buy some magazines, say ten. Find and cut out pictures related to your problem/solution, at least fifty

---

13   Robert Keith Sawyer, *Zig Zag: The Surprising Path to Greater Creativity* (San Francisco: Jossey-Bass, 2013).
14   Quote attributed to Thomas Edison.

of them, and make a collage near your desk in order to visualize it every day for a couple of weeks. This is only one example, but you have to find your own way to take into consideration the feasibility and implementation of your ideas.

Creative Techniques

As I explained earlier, creativity is seldom the result of hard thinking about finding an innovative solution; rather it is the consequence of having a "creative rhythm." Several techniques have been defined and tested. Many of them imply redefining either the problem or the context. The following techniques have been gathered from several sources mentioned in this book, in particular from the book *Thinkertoys*[15] by Michael Michalko and from Ramon Vullings's website.[16]

CHALLENGE ASSUMPTIONS

To overcome your thinking patterns, list the underlying assumptions related to your problem and challenge them one by one asking "what if it is not true?" You can also completely reverse these assumptions even if they seem evident, fundamental, or solid by writing down the exact opposite. Then you have to think about how to accomplish each reversed assumption. For example, look at the disruption in the world of music made by Spotify. Here the assumption was "people pay to access songs." The reverse was "people don't pay to access songs" and the next step was to think about how to accomplish this reversal—in the case of Spotify, it was to make advertisers pay for the songs or pay a subscription for all available songs instead of paying for single songs or albums.

Imagine, for example, that you work for a low-cost airline company and you have to study how to increase the number of customers. You have a strong assumption that your client base is quite price sensitive and you start analyzing price elasticity and creating simulations to determine how many customers you can gain by lowering the price. However, it seems that demand can't increase so much as to compensate for the lower price. In this case, you may challenge the assumption and assume

15 Michael Michalko, *Thinkertoys: A Handbook of Creative-Thinking Techniques* (New York: Ten Speed Press, 2006).
16 http://www.ramonvullings.com/free-downloads/

that your customers are not price sensitive. At this point, you can either simulate a price increase or modify other aspects of the offer.

Another way to challenge the underlying assumptions is to change the wording of the sentence that represents your problem. For example, suppose you have this problem: "Surveys show that the perception of the price-quality relationship of product X is dropping worryingly." In the beginning, you focus your attention on "quality," since you believe that the main cause of the problem must lie there as the prices have not changed. You may move the focus to another word—for example, "perception"—so perhaps the real quality did not drop but people believed that it has worsened. Or "surveys," so perhaps the survey is biased for some reason, for example, because it was taken when you had issued a series of defective products Y, and many of those who bought product X also bought product Y, so the discontent for the other product generated a general negative feeling.

IDEA DEVELOPMENT

Leonardo da Vinci would have tackled a problem through *mind mapping*, where you map out your thoughts and impressions on a blank sheet starting from the big question (the challenge). Then you start writing keywords representing concepts and relate them to each other. It is during the process of connecting, clustering, grouping, and regrouping keywords into concepts that creative ideas emerge. The theory behind this technique is that by randomly expressing words, your brain is not limited by some logical process and then, by associating them, your brain is forced to mix divergent patterns or pathways, producing creative ideas.

For example, suppose you have to identify the main drivers of customers' recommendation for a hotel chain. Using mind mapping, you would start by putting your "problem" at the center—"customers' recommendation"—and write keywords around it: "price," "service quality," "loyalty program," "incentives for recommendation," and so forth. Then you expand your main keywords by adding details; for instance, for "service quality" you can write "rooms," "restaurant," "reception," and so forth.

You first go on following this process until you think no further detail would significantly improve the information on the board. At this point, you should perform several iterations where you group similar concepts, eliminate redundant ones, and create associations. In this example you may think that "price" and "service quality" are related as the final recommendation will depend on a sort of price-quality relationship. Using this process, you might discover new associations you had not thought about. Finally, you may write down several questions for a customer survey from the mind map, gather enough responses, and test the correlation of recommendation with other variables you included in the survey (satisfaction about the reception service, how customers consider your price, etc.).

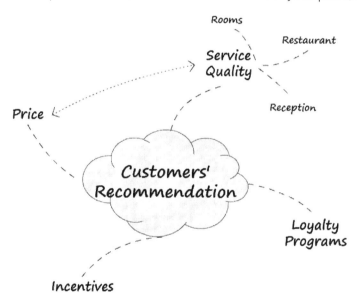

Figure 2: Example of mind mapping

A more structured alternative to mind mapping is the "Lotus Blossom Technique," where you start with a central theme or problem and you work outward generating eight ideas from this central one, and from each of these eight ideas, you create eight new ideas (see figure 3). Try to complete as much of the diagram as you can and then evaluate the ideas. Using the abovementioned example, you start by writing in the center "Customers' recommendation" and around it the main keywords (price, service quality, loyalty programs). Using this technique, you are in a certain way forced to find eight subcategories each time, so you are pushing yourself to think about all the possibilities. This exercise can help you explore some ideas you would have otherwise omitted.

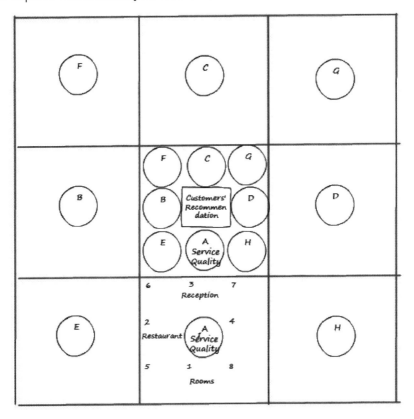

Figure 3: Example of Lotus Blossom Technique

RELAXATION

Sometimes it is useful to stop hard thinking and go to a quiet environment, stay in a comfortable position, empty your mind and relax, or you can just do something different distracting your mind from thinking about a problem. This technique is useful, as interrupting your current train of thoughts and "unfocusing" on a problem allows your brain to liberate different pathways. In addition, by engaging in a different activity, the use of senses instead of reasoning (touch, taste, etc.) can stimulate the right part of your brain.

Srini Pillay[17] defends the advantages of "unfocusing" the mind. Focus is very important in order to effectively and efficiently undertake a more or less complex set of tasks. However, too much focus can have negative effects, namely exhausting our brain energy with a consequent loss of control and more impulsive behavior. You should use a balance of focus and unfocus to enhance creativity. When you unfocus, your brain starts going back and forth among different memories and recombining. This increases your self-awareness and sense of personal relevance. Through unfocusing, you can imagine creative solutions, predict the future, make better decisions, and better understand other people. To implement this technique you can start doing a "low-key" activity such as gardening, cleaning, or relaxed reading. Then imagine something wishful and playful, for example running in the woods or laying on a beach. At this point, switch your attention from the external world to the internal space without stopping your low-key activity.

Sometimes this pause can be a bit longer to exploit the advantages of procrastination when used strategically. Usually, procrastination is seen as being *against* creativity since best practices are about acting right now and avoiding postponing perpetually what you have to do. However, Adam Grant in his book *Originals*[18] suggests that you can use it strategically when you are stuck and cannot move forward. In these situations, you can leave the task unfinished until the last moment. During this period, this reasoning will be alive in your subconscious and this may provoke sudden strokes of great ideas. This technique is based on the

---

17 Srini Pillay, "Brain Can Only Take So Much Focus," *Harvard Business Review* (May 2017); Srinivasan S. Pillay, *Tinker Dabble Doodle Try: Unlock the Power of the Unfocused Mind* (New York: Ballantine Books, 2017).

18 Adam Grant and Sheryl Sandberg, *Originals: How Non-Conformists Move the World* (New York: Penguin Publishing Group, 2017).

"Zeigarnik effect," according to which when we leave important tasks unfinished, the tension in our brain continues and the idea stays alive.

DIFFERENT PERSPECTIVES

Invented by Edward De Bono, the "Six Thinking Hats" technique aims at separately addressing different aspects of the problem. This prevents us from underestimating some of them and forces us to see the problem from different perspectives. More specifically, this technique tackles an issue by analyzing it from different points of view such as logical, emotional, or negative. Usually, each person is assigned a different perspective, and they are asked to develop an argument coherent with their perspective. For example, if someone has the negative hat, he or she will identify all the cons, problems, obstacles etc. related the issue. Besides, to better visualize the different perspectives, each person/perspective has a hat with a specific color. The symbolic act of assigning a specific color to them is a strategy to objectively analyze each of them (avoiding that the strongest aspect affects the analyses of the other ones). Suppose you are asked to evaluate why your premium product is not selling as well as your standard product and what aspects we can improve to sell it more:

- White: This is the fact-driven perspective and when you wear this hat you look at the problem with an analytical, logical, and mathematical point of view. Example: *"Since over time we changed the price of these two products, we can analyze the price sensitivity of consumers and identify the optimal price gap between the two in order to maximize revenues."*
- Green: The issue is tackled with a futuristic point of view, using creativity to suggest unusual and provocative ideas. This is when you leave space for pure creative thinking, for example considering other possibilities or alternatives. Here, you can use several creative thinking tools. Example: *"We should make several experiments to test the reaction of consumers, not only changing*

prices, but also introduce a third product, or selling only one of the two products for a certain period, or we can even reinvent both products."

- Yellow: With this hat, you have to look at the problem from a positive point of view, reasoning why it will be solved (or in case of an idea, why it will work). Example: *"With some adjustments we can improve sales of our premium version; probably we just have to increase the perceived difference between them to justify the premium price."*

- Black: It is used to criticize the proposed idea (or vision of the problem) by identifying all the barriers, issues, and details that are against it. It is quite a pessimistic perspective, but a very valuable one. This hat has to be used only in specific times, for example when you need to assess an idea, but avoid using it excessively and being negative all the time. Example: *"Analyzing current data you can't understand consumers' price sensitivity since there are many other factors affecting their choices, experiments are quite expensive and introducing some changes can produce negative reactions by our customers. Probably, the simple reason is that there is not enough demand for our premium product and we should just stop producing it."*

- Red: With this hat, you explore the emotional aspect of the problem using intuition and feelings instead of logic. Example: *"We must talk to our clients, not only with surveys, but in person and ask them why they chose one or the other product, to understand the real reason of their choices."*

- Blue: Overview, control, and recap are performed using the blue hat. Example: *"Even if there is a possibility that there is not enough demand for our premium product, it is worthwhile to explore all possibilities before giving up. Some experiments can be expensive, but we can propose some that imply little risk and cost, such as planning specific and limited price changes during the next few months. With this new data, we can enrich the price sensitivity analysis. It is also important to undertake some in-depth interviews to qualitatively explore the real reasons for customers' purchases. With better price-sensitivity information and new insights thanks to in-depth interviews, we can perform a conjoint analysis through an online survey to current and potential customers."*

You can use a different sequence, depending on the needs, but you can use the proposed one as a creative process per se. Before starting, make sure everybody has understood the concept. Use sheets of paper with the hat colors and the main characteristics of each one.

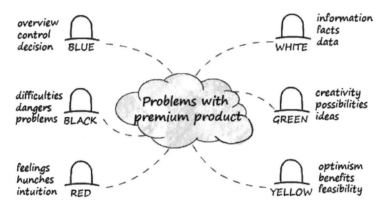

Figure 4: Example of Six Thinking Hats

The "Reframing Matrix" tool was first introduced by Michael Morgan.[19] It helps solve problems by examining them from different perspectives. You have to put yourself (or your team) in the shoes of different people and think about solutions. There are two main approaches to it. The first one is to formulate your problem (e.g., "new product not selling well") and look at it from four different perspectives:

---

19 Michael Morgan, *Creating Workforce Innovation: Turning Individual Creativity into Organizational Innovation* (Warriewood, NSW, Australia: Business & Professional Pub., 1993).

- Product: Issues concerning the product, service, or program itself, for example, whether it has some defects or if it did not work in the past.
- Planning: Issues related to business strategies and tactics.
- Potential: Is it scalable? Is it replicable?
- People: What customers (and/or other stakeholders) think about it?

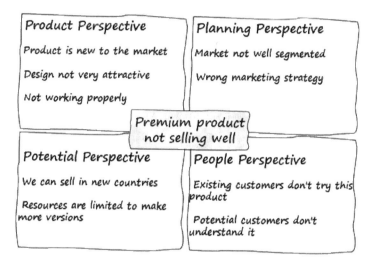

Figure 5: Example of Reframing Matrix tool

The second approach concerns viewing the problem from the point of view of different stakeholders (e.g., directors, sales managers, customers, developers, etc.)—thinking about how each of them would perceive the problem, how important it is for them, and with which solutions they would come up.

RANDOM INPUT

The brain is quite good at creating connections even with what would seem the most unlikely terms. We can use this property to form connections between random words, which would be unimaginable if you start from logical terms. You can invent whatever method for random inputs, for example, writing 50 words on slips of papers and then choosing them randomly. Once you choose a random word, you start creating a connection with the issue you are dealing with. The same logic works using objects, pictures, and so forth. In general, it is better if you use words that represent physical objects rather than concepts, and words that are not related to the field of the issue you are dealing with.

Take for example the phrase used before—"Surveys show that the perception of the price-quality relationship of product X is dropping worryingly"—and you add "tree." Tree can be associated with nature/green (make the product more natural to justify a high price), many species (differentiate the product to better fit customers' needs), and so forth. You can also add an adjective, for example, "bigger." This has to make you change the context of the problem by thinking for example that this negative perception is not due to the product itself, but it is something related to the image of the company or the brand.

BRAINSTORMING

Tom Kelley, general manager of IDEO, explains in his book *The Art of Innovation*[20] how to perform the "perfect brainstorm." First of all, it has to be done regularly (at least once a week) and it has to last less than one hour. It has to start with a clear definition of the problem and the facilitator has to obtain the attention and compromise of all participants (usually from four to eight) during all sessions. A good practice is to write down the topic on a flip board. It is recommended to assign a number to each idea, to write them down, and to visualize them using supporting materials like post-it notes (but avoid writing everything down, otherwise this will slow down the process and block ideas). The facilitator has to lead the conversation alternating moments when ideas flow freely and moments when he or she needs to intervene in order to move on the creative process (for example, when ideas stop to flow). In this case, the facilitator can

---

20 Tom Kelley, Jonathan Littman, and Thomas J. Peters, *The Art of Innovation: Lessons in Creativity from IDEO, America's Leading Design Firm* (London: Profile Books, 2016).

either focus on one or more ideas in order to improve them, or change the conversation completely, seeking a different kind of solution. In addition, the facilitator has to make the conversation flow smoothly, allowing everybody to talk without making them wait for their turn to speak (ideas can be forgotten or people may move on and start thinking something different). Criticism and judgment must be avoided during the phase of idea generation. In the end, the facilitator has to conclude the session by organizing the ideas (combining similar ones, grouping, clarifying, etc.) and obtain a consensus on which ideas should be looked at further.

A useful tool to organize ideas and to prevent forgetting them is the COCD Box (Center for Development of Creative Thinking). Basically, it is a matrix that organizes ideas by originality and ease of implementation. The ideas are organized into four groups, each with a different color. You can also use colored sticky notes and ask each member or group to generate ideas of different "colors."

Whether the data analyst is the facilitator or a group member, he or she has to be aware that in brainstorming, as in other group activities, three aspects have to be carefully managed: composition, participation, and influence.

In order to generate unbiased valuable solutions, it is important to have different perspectives in the group. However, groups have a tendency to be formed by similar people and this may undermine the results. Another problem is that sometimes decision makers include just experts in these groups, excluding different points of view that are valuable. To avoid this, group participants must be chosen carefully, taking into consideration the goal of the group session and the needed representativeness. Don't forget to also include people that will be affected by the results of the group session. Including these people (i.e., those who will implement the solution) not only means having a better understanding of the practical viability of an idea, but also facilitates the implementation since they feel part of the decision process.

If increasing the number of participants seems like a good thing for solving the composition problem, it also worsens the second aspect of group work: participation. The more people participate, the fewer people intervene, especially less predominant ones who become comfortable spectating. If the group is too large, you can split it into subgroups, and the representatives of each group will share the conclusions the group has agreed on. In this way, each member, even if not directly, participates. In addition, it is a good practice to make everybody talk at the beginning of the session as a psychological aid for shy people to share their ideas in the following part of the session.

Finally, people are naturally influenced by other people when sharing ideas. This prevents participants from expressing their own thoughts and perspectives, impoverishing results. Company members with higher positions, leaders, and influencers are those who can largely bias the interventions of other participants; therefore, it is advisable to allow them to speak last. Dissent must be fostered, especially against the opinion of the most influencing members. You can also ask participants to write down their own ideas before starting the session, making them stick more to their ideas and be less influenced by those of others.

Know the Business

To become a good data analyst, first, you must learn about the sector you are working in and the specificities of your company. Talk to people in different positions in your company, talk to suppliers and clients, go to events related to your sector, and read magazines, books, and blogs. A good practice is to set Google Alerts to find new online content related to your sector.

Having good knowledge of the business will help you in several aspects of your work. First, it will help you think strategically (see next chapter) when you have to define a new study or interpret the results of an analysis. Second, it is extremely useful to complement and double-check the results of models, forecasts, and so forth. For example, if your forecast tells you that your sales will double on the following weekend, but you know that sales are not going well in general for you and your competitors, you should revise your model.

I find it useful to organize the information using the components of the business environment. Personally, I like to visualize it by representing the entire business environment using three concentric layers:

- External macro-environment
- Competitive environment (external micro-environment)
- Internal environment

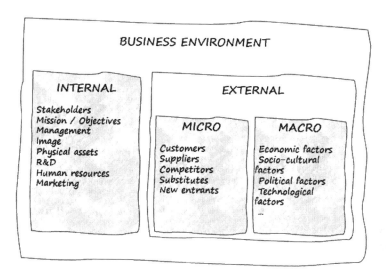

Figure 6: Business environment

The "external macro-environment" includes the external trends that impact the whole industry and, thus, your company. These trends are usually categorized across several areas, but the categorization is a mere facilitating element. I recommend the following categorization, with examples of trends affecting an airline company:

- Political trends: Change in visa restriction, political instability, increase in tourist taxes, etc.
- Economics trends: Increase in GDP per capita, economic crisis, etc.
- Socio-cultural trends: A destination that's become popular, new eco-friendly sentiment among people, etc.
- Technological trends: New lightweight material for aircraft building, etc.
- Environmental trends: Climate change, etc.

Being aware of these trends gives you a valuable qualitative understanding of external factors that may impact your company's results and will give you precious elements for anticipating the future.

Unfortunately, there is no precise process to obtain this information, but this is the result of keeping yourself up to date in these areas, particularly in what your industry and company are more concerned about. To achieve that, my suggestion is to talk to different people (inside and outside your company), to read articles, magazines, and blogs, and to attend to different events (conferences, trainings, workshops, etc.).

The "external micro-environment" includes those actors interrelated with your company and that form the competitive environment in which your company operates. We can use the model defined by Michael Porter (Porter's five forces)[21] as the starting point for analyzing this environment:

- Competitors: How strong is the rivalry among competitors?
- New entrants: How easy is it for new entrants to start competing?
- Substitutes: How many and how significant are they?
- Buyers: How many are there and how easily can they change suppliers?
- Suppliers: How many are there and how high are the switching costs for buyers?

These questions help you define your position in the competitive environment and complete the information on the external macro-environment.

---

21 Michael E. Porter, "How Competitive Forces Shape Competition," *Harvard Business Review* (March 1979).

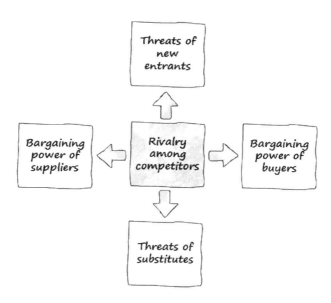

Figure 7: Porter's five forces of competition

I find it very intuitive to represent the "internal environment" by using the Business Model Canvas created by Alexander Osterwalder.[22] Here is the explanation from my previous book":

*First, we define our **customer segments** and then the **value propositions** that we are offering to them. The value proposition is a need that we satisfy or a problem that we solve for a specific customer segment. It is possible that we are offering different value propositions to different customers; for example, a search engine is providing search results to web users and advertising spaces to companies. Then we identify how to deliver this value to our customers (**channels**) and how we manage our relationships with them (**customer relationships**). At this point, we are able to describe our revenue model (**revenue streams**). However, to understand how to create our value propositions, we need to identify*

22 Alexander Osterwalder, Yves Pigneur, Tim Clark, and Alan Smith, *Business Model Generation: A Handbook for Visionaries, Game Changers, and Challengers* (Hoboken, NJ: Wiley, 2010).

*our **key activities, key resources,** and **key partners.** These three blocks allow us to identify our **cost structure.**[23]*

All blocks are interconnected; changes to one part affect the others. This reflects the dynamic nature of a business. Moreover, this model helps you adopt a broader strategic approach in understanding a business, without having to enter into operational details.

This Canvas is useful to analyze not only your company's business model, but also business models of your competitors.

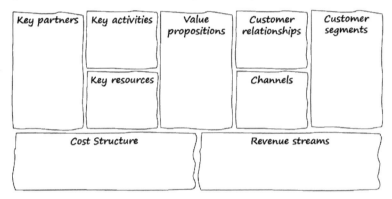

Figure 8: Business Model Canvas (by Alexander Osterwalder)[21]

You can also organize the information about your competitors in a "competitive map" where you compare your company with competitors according to several items. For each item-company you establish a score (according to your judgment or according to a survey) to graphically check your positioning in the sector. For example, if you are selling mobile phones you can compare price, general performance, users' satisfaction, battery duration, and so forth.

23 Alberto Scappini, *Fundamental Models for Business Analysts: Descriptive, Predictive, and Prescriptive Analytics Models with Ready-to-Use Excel Templates* (North Charleston, SC: CreateSpace, 2016), 80.

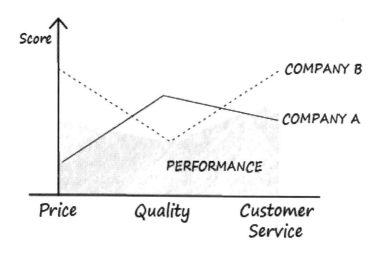

Figure 9: Competitive map

Think Strategically

S trategic thinking will make your analyses more effective and more efficient since it will help you focus your energy and efforts on what really matters. This is true not only when starting a study or analysis, but also during the process. In other words, you have to understand when you are incurring into "paralysis by analysis" and when the additional effort in refining the study is not worthy of the improvement in the results that you will eventually obtain.

Thinking strategically means that you are able to broaden your view on the problem and consider the interconnections between different elements—and not only focus on the details of an issue. For example, imagine you are estimating the price elasticity of your top clients and it turns out that your company can maximize revenues by increasing prices by 20%. If you are a strategic thinker, you should not stop there, but you should also consider the long-term consequences. Maybe this price increase will lower customer satisfaction, which is the main driver of your sales, and perhaps some of your top clients will finally switch to a competitor.

Thinking strategically also means that you can adapt to the new situation when necessary. You have to recognize the new or changing trends, challenge your first assumptions if necessary, and eventually modify the strategy you defined to reach specific goals.

You can't learn strategic thinking from a book, but I believe there are some interesting concepts that may help. These concepts concern both the content and the form of data analysis. On the one hand, to improve strategic thinking about the content of data analysis, you should master the basics of how businesses work. This refers basically to the subjects studied in MBA courses; they are of great help to see the big picture and identify important trends. On the other hand, strategic thinking about the form of data analysis includes having a global data strategy and adopting a strategic approach to data analysis.

Business Concepts

In this section, we will explore the main business concepts that I consider fundamental for a data artist to know. A great source of inspiration has been the book *The Personal MBA*,[24] which I strongly recommend you read, while some other concepts are derived from other business books. I am also going to try to relate all these concepts to each other and to the business environment, since in my experience this enhances the capability of retaining and understanding them.

VALUE CREATION

The essence of business is making someone else's life better in exchange for something—usually money—in a way that the business gains enough money to sustain operations and make profits. So, the first critical part is to create something that has value for the customer (something that satisfies a need or solves a problem). People make choices based on *five core drives*:

- To acquire: The desire of owning things, material and immaterial because they give you social status, power, etc.
- To bond: The desire to be loved and valued, for example, participating in conferences or meeting friends at a restaurant
- To learn: The desire to satisfy curiosity and be more knowledgeable
- To defend: The desire to feel or be able to defend yourself, for example, a self-defense course or installing an alarm in your house
- To feel: The desire to feel emotions and experiences

Usually, products and services provide a combination of these drives, which represents "what" a customer needs. However, eventually, the

---

24   Josh Kaufman, *The Personal MBA: Master the Art of Business* (New York: Portfolio/Penguin, 2012).

customer will be valuating different alternatives based on the perceived *economic value of your offer.* Usually, businesses have to tradeoff between two different groups of elements that form the economic value:

- Convenience, which includes elements such as speed, reliability, ease of use, and flexibility
- Fidelity, which includes elements such as status, aesthetic appeal, and emotion

The last element is the cost of your offer, which tends to be lower in high-convenience offers and higher in high-fidelity offers. Simplifying, in the first case you are more inclined to offer little value for a large majority of people (since your margins are low, you need more people to buy your product), while in the latter case you produce high value for a limited number of people. However, if your company is going to pursue a "Blue Ocean Strategy," it will have to seek both differentiation and low cost to disrupt the market (see box 2).

In the past, in order to sustain costs of production and distribution, regardless of whether you chose a convenience or fidelity positioning, you needed to reach a critical mass to be profitable. However, nowadays the cost of production and distribution is constantly reducing, allowing a lot of niche products to enter the market. Take, for example, the music industry where the share of top songs has diminished in favor of smaller singers who can easily record and distribute their songs. This democratization of production tools and the reduction of costs (at least in certain sectors) have generated several niche markets that overall are as important as the mass market for the few top-selling products (Box 1: The Long Tail).

Box 1: The Long Tail[25]

The long tail is a statistical curve that represents the distribution of sales of different products; in the head you have the famous ones sold to the masses, while in the tail you find almost an infinite quantity of products that sell to niches.

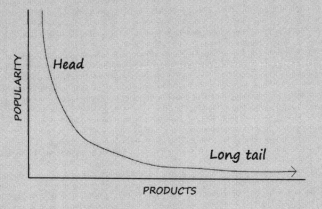

Figure 10: The long tail

One of the best examples to explain this phenomenon is music. In the 70s and 80s, you had a limited number of mega hits. However, in 2003 Apple launched the iTunes Music Store, allowing customers to access many more songs not limited by the shelf space of physical music stores. Besides, it allowed people to buy single songs instead of the entire album. Another important change was the almost "zero" reproduction and distribution costs since there was no more need for a physical support for the songs (CDs).

On the production side, independent artists could more easily and less expensively access the production tools, allowing them to produce songs even without a record company. Then, a few years later, Spotify appeared and expanded the access of songs even further, making access to the market for niche songs even easier. In addition to this, for these niche songs to find listeners, the role of

---

25 Chris Anderson, *The Long Tail: How Endless Choice Is Creating Unlimited Demand* (New York: Random House Business, 2009).

other customers—who help them find those songs by creating playlists and by their mere activity of following artists, playlists, or listening songs—becomes quite important.

The long tail phenomenon is also important for product aggregators such as Amazon. Take books, for example. Amazon is offering best-selling books from famous artists, as well as niche books produced by independent writers. It even offers editing tools writers can use to publish their books. At the end of the day, even if these independent authors sell just a few books each, the sum of them makes this market as important as those of the few top-selling writers.

Suppose you are producing cars. You have defined a new car that satisfies the need of moving from A to B, but which is also a high-fidelity product that satisfies the desires of status and power. Now you have to determine how to exchange your offer for money, or, in other words, which *form of value* you want to assign to it. In this case, you may want your customer to opt for ownership (product form of value), where your customer takes ownership of the car in exchange for a sum of money. But you may also offer other options such as leasing. Other forms of value are service, shared resources (you charge for the use of the product), subscription, resale (what retailers do), agency (you are paid for putting buyers and sellers into contact with each other), audience aggregation (this is what magazines do when they sell advertising spaces), loan, option (for example theater tickets, where you buy the option to do something during a specific period of time), insurance, and capital (purchase of an ownership stake in a business).

These different forms of value can be combined to increase the economic value; for example, a magazine can use subscriptions for its readers, and audience aggregation for advertisers. You can also increase the perceived value for a customer by *bundling or unbundling* an existing offer. For example, you can bundle several services when selling a mobile phone (the physical product itself, internet access, minutes of calls included, etc., all for a monthly fee) in order to increase the perceived value and make the customer willing to pay more, or to improve the offer compared to competitors. The opposite is unbundling and it can be useful to make a product valuable for a group of customers that otherwise wouldn't have bought it. For example, if instead of selling the full CD of ten songs, you allow customers to buy single songs, you may attract new customers.

A good offer that properly satisfies some need is not enough. You need a sufficiently big market to make your offer profitable. As a rule of thumb, you can have the first assessment on how attractive your target market is by answering the following questions on a 0 to 10 scale:

- How urgent is it to get your offer? For example, the last match in a football stadium before it gets demolished has high urgency
- How big is the market?
- What is the pricing potential? How much can you charge?
- What is the cost of acquiring new customers?
- What is the cost of delivering your offer?
- How unique is your offer?
- How quickly can you create your offer to be sold?
- How much investment is needed before you start selling?
- What is the upsell potential?
- After the initial sale, how much does it cost to continue operating?

You can also evaluate the target market by *learning from the competition*. Become their customer to learn how they produce value, how they price products, how they relate with their customers. In spite of what may seem logical, when you have to choose a market, you better choose the one with competitors. Where there is competition there is demand. However, this may not be true in mature markets where profits are declining. You may enter an existing market but if demand is not sufficient for you and your competitors, you will have to purse a "Blue Ocean Strategy," leaving the highly competitive red ocean in search of a blue ocean (see box 2).

Box 2: Blue Ocean Strategy

Adopting a "Blue Ocean Strategy" means you stop competing against your competitors by making them irrelevant.[26] If you compete with them, you are in a crowded red ocean where companies are fighting to increase their market share. However, you can disrupt the market by changing the underlying paradigms and finding blue oceans where the potential of growth is huge. To do so, you must focus on value innovation, offering your customers features that have never been offered earlier at a reasonable price. For example, Apple disrupted the music industry by introducing the iPod and iTunes; then Spotify did the same, just after seven years. Unlikely common positioning strategy, value innovation is the result of both differentiation and low-cost strategies.

More practically, to innovate you can start by analyzing the attributes of your competitors' products. Rate their performance to understand on what they are currently investing and against what they are mainly competing. Don't just include competitors in this analysis; also include substitutes (alternative products that fulfill the same need or solve the same problem). The key question here is "What can I do to make noncustomers buy?"

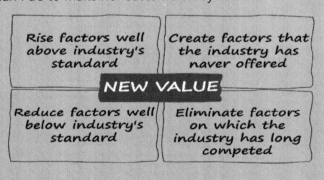

Figure 11: Strategy Canvas (Blue Ocean Strategy)

26 W. Chan Kim and Mauborgne Renée, *Blue Ocean Strategy: How to Create Uncontested Market Space and Make the Competition Irrelevant* (Boston, MA: Harvard Business School Press, 2005).

The next step is to study which are the factors currently taken for granted that you can drastically change:

1. Which factors on which the industry has long competed can be eliminated?
2. Which factors can be reduced well below the industry's standard?
3. Which factors can be raised well above the industry's standard?
4. Which factors that are never offered by the industry can be created?

Coming back to the example of Apple, it disrupted the industry by raising exponentially the number of songs you can bring with you in a significantly smaller device, and it created the possibility to legally buy a single song instead of an entire album. Now with Spotify, you can even listen to songs for free (if you accept advertising and pauses) and with an internet connection, there is almost no limit to the number of songs you can bring with you.

There are four key principles in developing a Blue Ocean Strategy:

1) Reconstruct market boundaries: Among many possible blue oceans, you have to find the viable ones. The key is to look at familiar data but from different perspectives. You can look across alternative industries (Cirque du Soleil did it by creating something between circus and entertainment), different groups of customers, different groups of competitors, or complementary products (Starbucks changed the emphasis on selling coffee to selling experiences). Another alternative is to make a functional product more emotional, or an emotional product more functional.

2) Focus on the big picture: Instead of creating a detailed strategic plan, draw up your company's strategy canvas. This will help you focus on the big picture rather than operational details.

3) <u>Reach beyond existing demand</u>: The bigger the market, the smaller the risk. For this reason, you have to try going beyond the current customer base and reaching different levels of "noncustomers." To attract them, use the communalities they have among them and with your customers to remove barriers to purchase.

4) <u>Get the strategic sequence right</u>: First of all, you have to offer exceptional utility to the customer. Second, define a fair price that can attract the mass market instead of charging a premium for the first adopters. This will help you build a robust customer base and spread the voice. Third, make it profitable starting with the price and subtracting the margin you require. If you do this, you will have to adapt your costs for example by changing production methods. Finally, the product must be adopted easily. Start with employees and business partners before offering the product to the general public.

Also remember that execution is extremely important and even if you find a viable blue ocean but you do not properly execute your strategy, you will fail.

When evaluating the possibility of a new business, or evaluating the results (bad results!) of a new product or start-up, consider reassessing your *underlying assumptions*. For example, your assumption for opening a new restaurant was that people will be willing to pay 50€ per meal since you are in a good neighborhood and because you offer quality food. However, you discovered that you were wrong, and people are only willing to pay 40€. This creates a problem in your second assumption, according to which you are able to sell 100 meals a day. With 40€ meals, you are selling 100 meals a day, but this is not enough to reach your expected daily revenues of 5,000€ that are necessary to cover costs and make some profit.

For this reason, besides carefully evaluating assumptions, you should test the market. Instead of asking what people want (they will say they want everything for free!), ask them about the *relative importance of the attributes of your offer* (quality, price, number of meals offered, etc.). For example, you can propose four to five attributes and ask them to choose the most and least desired. It is even better if you can ask them to choose among several combinations of attributes.

However, even if you force them to choose the most desirable attributes, it is not equivalent to purchasing your product for real. It is a good practice to do some *shadow testing* by giving the possibility to preorder the product to test the real purchase intention. Another option to test this is to create a *prototype*—that is a simpler version of your offer but with enough attributes to represent it and to obtain valuable feedback. It doesn't have to be perfect, but the more realistic, the better. This is also called "minimum economically viable offer," thanks to which you receive valuable feedback and choose whether and how to develop it. You should become your own customer, as using your own products will help to improve them (*field testing*).

When you have a good value proposition and you have concluded that there is enough demand, you have to develop and improve your offer through *iterative cycles* (observe, ideate, guess, modify, act, and measure). The best way to do this is to keep iterations small, quick, and clear to incrementally improve your offer. During this phase, you will have to face several *trade-offs*, since you can't implement everything due to budget limitations or contraposing attributes (for example, cheap and high quality often can't go together). When you are considering several *alternatives*, try to think of alternatives your customers are considering, find common patterns among them, and choose the most profitable ones. This concept is particularly important for data artists when defining the problem and the analytical project, since it often includes the prioritization of recommendations.

Finally, remember that when you are producing and improving your product, you don't' just have to rely on your internal resources (i.e., employees), but you can also be helped by consumers themselves. This concept of mass collaboration and networked intelligence transformed consumers into "prosumers," that is, consumers who are also involved in the production process (see box 3).

Box 3: Wikinomics[27]

Wikinomics defines the phenomenon of mass collaboration and net-worked intelligence. New tools and opensource information have been put at everyone's disposal and this has allowed different people to collaborate in different projects motivated by personal need, social recognition, or just for the personal satisfaction of contributing to something bigger. "The example," from which comes the name "Wikinomics", is Wikipedia, where millions of users contribute to increase and improve the world's biggest encyclopedia.

Five forces shape the concept of Wikinomics:

1. Collaboration: Companies' borders are blurring and they rely increasingly on external human capital to acquire new ideas and benefit from collaborative innovation.
2. Openness: Companies tend to disclose information that was once considered sensitive. In addition, in this era of collaboration, people demand more transparency and honesty.
3. Sharing: More information is shared, including important assets such as intellectual property or software codes to make pro-sumers work on them and improve them.
4. Integrity: Thanks to openness, good behavior will automatically reward companies' reputations.
5. Interdependence: Due to increasing collaboration, there will be a greater number of connections.

MARKETING

A valuable offer alone doesn't sell for itself, but potential customers need to be aware that it exists and about its benefits. Marketing means getting the attention of customers whose needs can be fulfilled with your offer, deliver to them a convincing message about why you offer the best

---

27 Don Tapscott and Anthony D. Williams, *Wikinomics: How Mass Collaboration Changes Everything* (New York: Portfolio, 2010).

solution, and call them to action. The final purpose is to convert them into buyers.

First, you have to focus only on *probable purchasers*—on those people suited for what you are selling and whose needs can be fulfilled with your product. Look for the deepest needs, focus on the *end result* of what a customer really wants from a product or service. For example, the real motivation for paying for an MBA may be prestige, rather than learning. In this case, the reputation of the school is far more important than the kind and quality of courses taught. Even if it is easier to work on product features, try to go further and understand the real desires of potential customers. And if you want to go even further, you should focus on *qualified potential customers*, namely those who are likely to be profitable for the company since they generate more revenues than the cost they cause (time, customer service, devolutions, discounts, etc.).

Once your target is defined, you have to reach these potential customers. In some cases, it may be more difficult than others, for instance, if the needs or problems are embarrassing—since people tend not to show them and not group with other people with similar problems to talk about them. This concept is called *addressability* and it defines how easy it is to reach your target. In any case, you have to get the limited *attention* of these people by finding a way around to the many filters they use to select what and when something is worthy of their attention. So you have to be more interesting and useful than alternatives and choose the right time to try to get their attention. Choosing the right time not only means the right moment during the day or week, but also to try to get customer attention right after the need arises (called *point of market entry*) to become the point of reference and increase the impact. For example, you should impact tourists when their desire to travel to a certain destination arises. To acquire quality attention from potential customers, it is recommended to ask *permission* to contact them (or to give more information, make an offer, etc.) instead of interrupting, since in the latter case rejection tends to be higher (see box 4).

Box 4: Permission Marketing[28]

Nowadays, consumers are overwhelmed by gimmick advertisements that aim at interrupting them in order to catch their attention. For this reason, attention is becoming increasingly scarce and the effectiveness of interruption marketing is constantly diminishing. Seth Godin proposes a different approach called "permission marketing," which means that you ask customers for permission in order to give them information about your product and, eventually, ask to buy it. Gaining consumers' consent to participate in a selling process establishes long-term relationships between the company and the client, improving trust and loyalty.

Permission marketing increases customers' attention because they are participating voluntarily in the process. However, your message must be anticipated, personal, and relevant to obtain customers' permission.

To achieve customers' consent, follow these steps:

1. Offer a reason for a potential customer to get voluntarily involved (i.e., give relevant information, incentives, bonuses, etc.).
2. Give more and more information about the product to sustain their attention.
3. Maintain and reinforce incentives, and ask for permission to give more information.
4. Gain more permission to continue the relationship.
5. Eventually, use the permission to sell.

28 Seth Godin, *Permission Marketing: Turning Strangers into Friends, and Friends into Customers* (New York: Simon & Schuster, 1999).

Depending on the kind of business and the opportunities, there are five main levels of permission:

1. Intravenous level: You make purchasing choices on behalf of your customer (e.g., a grocery that makes regular delivery to its clients since the seller chooses the vegetables for the client).
2. Points permission level: For example, the miles that airline companies give to customers who can redeem them to buy future flights.
3. Personal relationship level: It depends on the personal contact between the customer and a salesman, usually employed for the sale of expensive products or services.
4. Brand trust level: Related to the "old approach," the company tries to build trust through a brand.
5. Situation level: In each contact situation with the customer, the company can try different approaches to ask for permission.

To increase your chances to get attention, you can act on three main elements: product, price, and message. If you have a really *remarkable product* (such as the FiveFingers shoes), it will generate attention thanks to the word-of-mouth of customers and will stand out from the competitors (see box 5).

Box 5: Purple Cow

According to Seth Godin,[29] in a world with ever-increasing available choices and ever decreasing time, it is not enough to produce an average product for the masses and then buy a lot of advertising to sell it. You have to start by creating a really remarkable product, which will stand out by its own characteristics and not thanks to advertising. You have to create something like a purple cow among millions of conventional cows.

---

29 Seth Godin, *Purple Cow: Transform Your Business by Being Remarkable* (New York: Penguin, 2005).

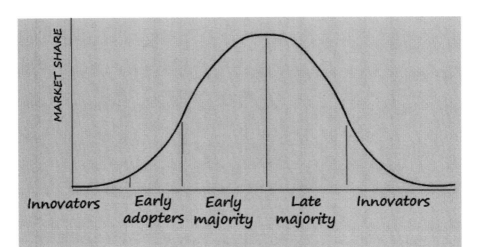

Figure 12: Moore's idea diffusion curve

Your idea will move through a market, starting with innovators, who are eager to risk experimenting something new because they want to be the first ones. Then you have early adopters who want to maintain their edge on the rest of the population by adopting relatively new products. Then there are the early and late majorities, who will be interested in your products if early adopters had sufficiently and convincingly spread your idea. These people will ignore you unless their peers talk about you, so don't create a product for the market, but create a really remarkable product for a specific niche that is eager to listen to you. Then the main challenge is that the product must be so remarkable that will make those early adopters eager to spread your idea to the rest of the curve (Moore's idea diffusion curve).

If your product is not so remarkable, you may try by giving if for *free*. Low prices can generate some attention, but giving something valuable for free is far more effective. But avoid giving free stuff just for getting attention, since finally it is a cost and you have to transform these prospects into real paying customers (see box 6).

Box 6: Free

With production costs constantly decreasing, "free" is no longer just an attention-grabbing technique, but a valuable business model.[30] This is particularly true in the digital economy where the costs of producing and distributing an additional unit are practically zero. According to the old business model, the more scarce you make your product, the more valuable it will be. However, the digital economy changed this paradigm from a scarcity economy to an abundance economy: infinite shelf space, copies made and distributed at zero cost, a huge number of distribution channels, and so forth.

There are four main business models for Free:

1. Direct cross-subsidy: A free product is given to the consumer (loss leader) in order to generate sales for other products. An example of loss leader is when a supermarket is selling a product at a price below its production cost in order to attract customers who will hopefully also buy other products.

2. Three-party markets: This is the model used by media, for example when the newspaper is given for free while advertisers pay for the advertising space. The circle is closed when consumers buy the advertised products. If you are distributing news for free, you can reach a larger circulation, allowing you to charge more for advertising. However, the quality of the public can be lower than for a paying newspaper. Probably the most successful example nowadays is Google, which gives free services to internet users, while charging advertisers for reaching the most probable purchasers.

3. Freemium: This is widely used online for services or software, where you can get the basic version for free, but if you want the better version you have to pay. The advantage of offering a free basic version is that you can reach many prospective

---

30 Chris Anderson, *Free: How Today's Smartest Businesses Profit by Giving Something for Nothing* (New York: Hyperion, 2010).

premium customers and you can make your service the reference in a specific domain. Examples are Business Intelligence tools (Tableau, QlikView, or Power BI) which are offering free basic versions.

4. Nonmonetary markets: In some models, the producer gives the service or product for free because the gains are not monetary, that is, reputation, attention, satisfaction. Wikipedia is an example.

However, just giving away free stuff doesn't mean you're succeeding. You have first to acknowledge this reality, understand how it works, and build a business model around free. You must have a clear plan about how to monetize it after giving away something for free. Use free to reach the masses, to get attention or reputation, and then develop your "paid" business model on them. For example, when Radiohead released "In Rainbows," they made it available for download asking the customers to pay what they considered fair (including nothing!). The result was an extremely successful album. This success allowed them to sell a deluxe boxed version of the album at a premium price, to sell more CDs, and to make their tour more profitable.

Finally, you must work carefully on your message. First, since it cannot be too large, you have to "frame" it by choosing the most important details, namely the most important benefits of the offer. The best way a message can get attention and be remembered is by making it a *hook*. It means using a single short phrase that communicates the most important benefit in a remarkable way. An example is the iPod message "1,000 songs in your pocket." It brilliantly conveys the main benefits of the iPod versus CD and cassette players (the device is so small that it fits into a pocket with almost unlimited songs). Ideally, your message should reach the "Tipping Point" from which it spreads like a virus among potential consumers (see box 7).

Box 7: The Tipping Point31 and the Ideavirus32

The theory of the "tipping point" tries to explain how fashions and trends can spread so quickly and extensively among consumers. Ideas can be compared to diseases, which need a series of conditions to become epidemics—namely, the kind of disease itself, the people carrying them, and the context. Ideas too can be spread like viruses, but just having a good idea is not enough. First of all, your idea/product must be "virusworthy": it can get by itself the attention of people and it is so interesting that people will desire to spread it.

The idea has to be aimed initially at a specific target market, relatively small, and with a specific problem or need. But first, you need to reach a few people who will be responsible for spreading the idea. Seth Godin (*Unleashing the Ideavirus*) calls them "sneezers" and they can be categorized into two groups: powerful sneezers (whose opinion can't be bought and are trusted by people) and promiscuous sneezers (to whom you have to give incentives to get your idea spread, but even if their opinion is less valuable, they usually can reach a lot of people). Malcolm Gladwell instead divides them into three categories, all of them important for reaching the tipping point:

1. Connectors: They know a lot of people but they usually have weak ties.
2. Mavens: They like to accumulate information and knowledge, and pass them to other people.
3. Salespeople: They are able to persuade and generate trust since they are passionate and likable in the eyes of other people.

Besides the nuances, both authors agree on the fact that to make these people spread your idea, it must be about something new,

31 Malcolm Gladwell, *The Tipping Point: How Little Things Can Make a Big Difference* (Boston, MA: Little Brown, 2000).
32 Seth Godin, *Unleashing the Ideavirus: Stop Marketing AT People! Turn Your Ideas into Epidemics by Helping Your Customers Do the Marketing for You* (New York: Hachette Books, 2001).

outstanding, and compelling. They will spread your idea only if it is worthy, or, put another way, if spreading this idea will improve their social prestige and reputation.

Another critical factor is how easily your idea can be spread. A simple and catchy message will help, as well as the medium you use and how you "pack" your idea. Little details may have a huge impact on creating the "stickiness factor," which allows your idea to be spread. In addition to this, the speed and the direction with which your idea moves are important too.

Finally, it is very important to understand and properly manage the lifecycle of ideas, especially when they reach the highest point and you have to extend it. Trends and fashions can fade as quickly as they rocketed. This is why you have to be persistent and find a way to constantly amplify them.

Another way to make your message more powerful is to *tell a story.* People are fascinated by stories, which also have the benefit of being more easily remembered. In particular, they are fascinated by a specific kind of story, which starts with a "hero" who lives a normal life with normal everyday tribulations. However, out of the blue, the hero is faced with an extraordinary and difficult challenge that forces her or him out the normal life and for which he or she starts to train skills and capabilities to overcome the problem. During this remarkable experience, the hero learns many things and faces several adversities until the enemy is defeated. In the end, he or she returns to normal life with more power and is admired by everybody. In general, we are fascinated by stories where a normal person (like us!) can do extraordinary things and gain the admiration of other people, because we all want to be heroes. Customers are the same, so tell them an interesting, vivid, clear, and emotionally compelling story.

Controversy, that is taking a position with which many people will disagree, can also be used to make people start paying attention, engage, and talk about your offer. Josh Kaufman's "Personal MBA" project adopts a strong position that you don't need an MBA to learn how to do business. This is very controversial for business schools and for actual and former MBA students. However, this disagreement generated more discussions, and these discussions gained the attention of new people who started investigating this project.

Once you have the attention of potential customers, the goal is to make them take action: buy the product, tell a friend, subscribe to something, go to a specific place, and so forth. It is important that you include in your message a clear and simple *call-to-action*, which leads receivers toward what you want them to do. Keep in mind that you finally want potential customers to actually buy, so whichever action you suggest has to lead to that. On one side, the prospect will compare the features and price of what you offer versus several alternatives and will choose the best alternative according to her or his specific needs. On the other side, as I mentioned earlier, the end result is far more powerful than comparing features since it fulfills the real *desire* of people. If you are buying a car and your desire is "status," then you may not choose the car with the best features, but the one that will give you the best status, even in spite of the price. A successful technique that can awaken the preexisting desire of people is to make them *visualize* how their life will be after purchasing your product. Examples are a video about a tour package, a sample of face cream, the Apple store where you can try their products, or the test drive at a car dealer. All these examples have the power to make you imagine positive experiences, to awaken your feelings and desires, and finally, you will buy the product because you want it!

All your efforts of getting attention, delivering a good message, and calling people to action can be either magnified or undermined by *reputation.* For a company known for the quality of its cloth, it will be easier to communicate to prospects and convince them their product is better. However, if the company has the reputation of producing low-quality clothes, it will be far harder to deliver such a message. Reputation is a sort of guarantee that can lower the attention filters and make buyers trust the quality of the product without requiring much proof.

SALES

After creating value and making potential customers aware of it, you have to convert these prospects into paying customers. First, to reach a *transaction,* both parties must have minimum *trust* in each other. Second, they need to find a *common ground* where their interests are aligned. This means that the seller is willing to trade a product or service at a price the buyer is willing to pay for it. Determining the price is quite a challenging task due to the "pricing uncertainty principle," which depends on the demand, how much people are willing to pay, and how many alternatives they have. There are four main *pricing methods*:

- Replacement cost: Calculate the cost of an item and add a markup. This is probably the easiest way, although if you have important fixed costs you must carefully estimate the number of items that will be sold.
- Market comparison: Identify the price of alternatives and then adjust it for the differences.
- Discounted cash flow/net present value: For example, if you buy a house, you can calculate the discounted cash flow of future rents.
- Value comparison: Define the price based on people who have a higher willingness to pay.

When *defining customer's willingness to pay,* it is useful to differentiate between the price a person is willing to pay for a certain product and the price he or she is willing to pay considering the available alternatives. The second price is based on the price of your alternatives adjusted for the differences. The lower of the two prices will be the real willingness to pay of a potential customer.

The ideal situation for a seller is to set a personalized price based on the willingness to pay of each customer. However, usually, it may be only possible to set a different price for different clusters of customers. *Price discrimination* can be made by making customers choose among different deals, for example, quantity discounts or anticipated purchases. Another way is to select different groups of customers with different willingness to pay, for example offering a special price for students. An alternative way is to differentiate the basic product with specific characteristics and charge a different price. For example, the plus you pay for traveling in business class, or the discount you have if you book a hotel room with a nonrefundable and non-changeable offer.

Related to pricing, we have two main selling approaches. The first one aims at maximizing the price; it is called "value-based selling." This approach consists of setting the maximum price based on the reason why customers buy a certain item. To discover the real reason, you have to listen to customers, understand what their real needs are, and understand what they are willing to trade-off. You can play not only with price, but with the three *universal currencies* you have at your disposal: resources (physical staff), time, and flexibility.

The second approach is called "education-based selling" and in this case, you try to convince the customer that the offer is worth the price. This approach is suitable in situations where the customer lacks information or knowledge about the benefits of your offer and hence she or he has a lower willingness to pay.

Negotiation is an important part of sales. You can either negotiate directly or decide to use a *buffer* by empowering third parties to negotiate (agents, attorneys, etc.). This prevents you from worsening your reputation and allows you to gain space and time since these intermediaries don't have the final say. However, it is extremely important that your interests are aligned with those of the intermediaries.

In the negotiation, you can use the principle of *reciprocation*, according to which people have a common desire to give payback when someone gives them something. The interesting issue about this principle is that the payback does not have to be proportionate; at the start, you can give something small (e.g., a coffee, a free sample) to make the buyer feel the desire to give you something back by purchasing your product. In addition, you can convince the prospect to purchase by transferring part of all the risk to the seller. Examples of *risk reversal* are the "money back guarantees."

Another technique to increase your reputation and trust is to make *damaging admissions*, which means admitting to the customer the defects of the item you are trying to sell. Even if in principle you may think this is counterproductive, in reality, you are being honest with your customer and, if the defect is acceptable for the purchaser, he or she will think you are not hiding any major flaw.

Another important aspect of negotiation is to identify the existing *barriers to purchase* and make them either irrelevant or untrue. In general, you may find five main barriers:

- It costs too much: In this case, you have to better frame your offer highlighting why the value is worth the price.
- It won't work: Use social proof, testimonials or referrals.
- Ok, it works in general, but not for me: Use testimonials similar to your customer.
- I can wait: Use an education-based selling approach to explain why it can't wait.
- It's too difficult (it implies an effort for the buyer): Educate him or her that the benefits are worth the effort.

Finally, remember that in general, it is easier to make a former customer buy again than to find a new one (*reactivation*). This is because she or he has already shown interest in your product and you have important information about him, including contact information. All this makes the effort less costly.

VALUE DELIVERY

Once you have convinced a customer to buy your product, you have to deliver it to him or her as quickly, reliably, and consistently as possible to make the customer happy, to foster repeated purchases, and to improve your reputation. Generally speaking, a customer is satisfied if the performance of the product matches or exceeds his or her *expectations*.

Expectations should be high enough to convince him to buy and you may try to exceed them by giving a little unexpected bonus, such as free shipping, additional gadgets, and so forth.

If well-executed, value delivery can even become a competitive advantage. This advantage is "predictability" since customers and prospects will buy from you because they trust you to do the job right and on time. This will allow you to ask a premium price for the same service other competitors are offering. Think about how important it is nowadays for companies such as Amazon whose customers expect reliable and timely delivery. Predictability depends on three main factors:

- Uniformity: Deliver the same characteristics every time.
- Consistency: Deliver the same value over time.
- Reliability: Deliver on time.

To accomplish this, you have to carefully define your *value stream*, namely all the steps and processes necessary to deliver the end result to the customer. It is recommended to write it down or draw a clear diagram of it in order to *systemize*, examine, and improve it. This will also have other advantages, such as coordinating people involved in the process, automating the process, and focusing on improvement instead of on the operations.

However, to significantly improve it, it is not sufficient to draw it, but you must start measuring it. *Throughput* is the rate at which a system reaches a specified goal or the effectiveness of your value stream. The "unit throughput" is how much time it takes to sell an additional item, the shorter it is, the better.

The more customers you serve, the more important it will be to *scale* your value delivery. In the case of service businesses, the scalability is quite low since they rely heavily on human resources. Manufacturing has higher scalability, while digital products have almost infinite scalability. To scale your process, you can either *duplicate* the product you are producing or *multiply* it by duplicating the entire process. For example,

Starbucks duplicates its coffees for several clients. However, a single store has only a limited space for employees, machines, and clients so it multiplies the entire process by opening another store nearby. In addition to this, its machines *automate* some of the processes of producing coffee, further increasing the speed of the delivery.

You not only have to scale the value production, but also the final part of the value stream. Instead of only delivering directly to customers, you can also rely on intermediaries. These additional *distribution channels* exponentially increase your reach to potential customers. However, the drawbacks are that you lose direct contact with customers and important information about them. On top of that, if their quality of delivery is low, it can affect your reputation.

FINANCE

Finance is related to the money that flows into and out of the company, including the decisions on how to allocate them to finally generate enough margin to justify the time and energy invested. *Profit margin* is the key concept here, since a business sooner or later must generate more revenues than costs in a proportion that sufficiently compensate investors. To increase the margin, you can either increase revenues or diminish costs.

To *increase revenues,* you can implement several strategies, but in the end, you are acting on four main levers: number of customers, quantity sold per transaction, frequency of purchase, and prices. You can act on these levers to increase revenues, for example, you can offer a complimentary product (cross-selling) or buy a higher-quality product (upselling) to increase the quantity/value sold in a transaction.

You can also raise prices to maximize profits; however, since it has a negative effect on the number of customers or the frequency of purchase, it depends on your *pricing power*. It means that if customers are price sensitive (a concept known as "price elasticity of demand"), an increase in price will be negative on total revenues. On the other hand, if the demand is price inelastic (customers are not price sensitive), an increase in price will generate more revenues.

Alternatively, you can convince your existing customers to buy more often, or to continue their subscription as long as possible. This is one of the best levers to maximize your customers' *lifetime value*—that is, the long-term value of your existing customer base. Fostering repeated purchases allows you to save money on marketing efforts to attract new customers.

The lifetime value of a customer can be calculated using the following formula:

$$CLV = MC * \frac{r}{(1 + d - r)} - CA$$

CLV = customer lifetime value;

MC = yearly marginal contribution, that is the total purchase revenue in a year minus marketing and production costs;

r = retention rate (the probability for this customer to repeat the purchase next year, which can be simplified by using the % of recurring customers out of the total number of customers);

d = discount rate (since the money you will receive in the future is worth less than the money you receive now, you need to discount future earnings; you can use the cost of capital of your company);

CA = cost of acquisition (one-time cost spent by the company to reach a new customer).

Put simply, the value of a customer is the discounted sum of what he or she is going to spend in the future minus costs (production, marketing, etc.). You also have to subtract the cost of acquiring this customer that you incurred at the beginning. Besides more traditional business metrics, the importance of embracing a customer-centric strategy has created the need to use additional metrics, such as the ROC (return on customer). This metric measures the value created by acquiring, retaining, and growing your customer base (see box 8).

Box 8: Return on Customer

Return on customer (ROC)[33] is a measure of the present and future value of your customer base; it is calculated as follows:

$$ROC = \frac{\text{Current period cash flow} + \text{Change in customer equity}}{\text{Total customer equity at the beginning of this period}}$$

A positive ROC means you are increasing your customer base value, either by current cash flow or future earnings. If ROC is negative, you are eroding your customer equity or lifetime value.

Using ROC as a business performance metric will help you focus on your most scarce resource, that is, customers switching from a competition model to a model based on customer service. It helps to optimize the tradeoffs between short- and long-term profits finding the right balance. For example, you can lower the quality of your current product to increase your margin. But when you calculate the ROC, it will show that you are undermining customer retention and future sales. On the other hand, you cannot just focus on long-term profits because you may risk going out of business.

To improve customer equity, you have to consider the customer's perspective, that is understand what the real needs are. You can organize your customer base into different segments to personalize your product or service and to increase sales and customers' satisfaction. You should also segment your customers according to their lifetime value:

1. Most valuables: Focus on retaining them.
2. Most growables: These are those with an intermediate value but with a great growth potential. Focus on strategies that make them buy more often or increase the number and variety of products they buy.
3. Marginal valuables: Don't waste money on this segment since it usually won't be profitable.

33 Don Peppers and Martha Rogers, *Return on Customer: Creating Maximum Value From Your Scarcest Resource* (New York: Crown Business, 2005).

Another interesting concept related to the CLV is the CRV or the "customer referral value." Studies show that some customers may not be so valuable in terms of purchases, but they may be very valuable in recommending your product. The CRV is quite complicated to calculate due to the lack of available data (you must know who recommended to whom and whether he or she finally bought the product) but if you are interested in it, you can read the article "How Valuable Is Word of Mouth?"[34] published by the *Harvard Business Review*.

Finally, you can try to increase revenues by attracting more customers, which implies (if you are not going to lower your prices) investing more in marketing. The cost of conquering a new customer is called "acquisition cost" and, using the same concept of the CLV, we can calculate the *allowable acquisition cost*, which is the maximum cost you can spend to attract a new customer based on the estimated lifetime value:

$$AAC = \left(avg\ CLV - \text{Variable Costs} - \frac{Fixed\ Costs}{N.of\ customers}\right) * (1 - \%\ Profit\ Margin)$$

The allowable acquisition cost (ACC) is the lifetime value of a specific kind of customer minus variable costs, minus average fixed costs per customer, minus the % you pretend to earn in profits (1-% profit margin). This formula can be useful either to define how much to spend to attract a specific kind of customer or to verify whether the actual cost of acquisition is optimal. For example, your CLV is €1,000, your variable cost is €200, your fixed cost per customer is €300, and you want a minimum profit of 40%. Therefore, your calculation will look like this:

$$AAC = (1,000 - 200 - 300) * (1 - 40\%) = 300$$

This means that you can spend up to €300 to get a new customer.

I have explained so far some concepts about improving your profit margin by increasing revenues, but you can also do it by lowering costs. One option is to lower your *variable costs*—namely the costs you incur

---

to produce each item, and the more you produce, the higher the cost. By diminishing it, you will have a direct increase in the margin on each product sold. The other option is to reduce *fixed costs*—namely the costs you need to maintain your company on operations (rent, insurance, interest, etc.). Since these costs don't depend on production, the more you produce, the lower the cost per unit produced. *Semi-variable costs* (or semi-fixed costs) are those costs that don't vary until a certain amount of production is exceeded. For example, with the actual number of employees you may produce a maximum of X products per day; if you exceed this quantity, you will need more people.

Be aware that by reducing costs you can incur an *incremental degradation* of the value you are offering, increasingly eroding your *pricing power.*

As I explained at the beginning of this chapter, finance is also a matter of how to allocate money, that is, where to invest them. Whether you are creating a start-up or you are investing in a new product line, you will find the following concepts extremely useful.

First, you have to decide where to invest, since resources are limited and you need to choose the most profitable option. ROI may be considered the indicator "par excellence" of evaluating the worthiness of investing in a project.

$$ROI = \frac{(\text{Revenue from Investment} - \text{Cost of Investment})}{\text{Cost of Investment}}$$

First, evaluate whether it fulfills your minimum requirement for investments. Investing in a project means renouncing other investment opportunities (a concept known as *opportunity cost*); therefore, the return of this project must exceed the return of the best possible alternative. If no concrete alternative is on the table, you can use as the minimum requirement the cost of financing your activity (or the cost of borrowing money). Be careful when you are comparing alternatives with different levels of risk, since a riskier project will require a higher return. Bear in mind that you must not include in the calculation any *sunk cost*, that is what you have already spent and cannot be recovered. It doesn't matter if you have already spent a lot of money on a specific project, since you have to decide whether to continue with it, drop it, or choose another project, only based on the additional money you have to invest and the additional earnings.

Now suppose you are comparing two projects with the same ROI—for example, 20%—which one do you choose? The ROI has the limitation of not showing you the absolute value you are going to gain; this is why it is recommended to also calculate the NPV (net present value) of those projects. NPV is the present value (value discounted[35] at a certain discount rate "r") of future earnings minus future costs (net cash inflow "C_t"), minus the initial investment (C_0). The number of periods is represented by "t."

$$NPV = \sum_{t=1}^{T} \frac{C_t}{(1+r)^t} - C_0$$

According to the previous example, despite the fact that the two projects have the same ROI, you may choose the one with the highest NPV. If the amount of money varies in different periods, you will have to discount it separately. For that, I introduce the concept of "discounted cash flow" (DCF) here:

$$DCF = \frac{CF_1}{(1+r)^1} + \frac{CF_2}{(1+r)^2} + \frac{CF_n}{(1+r)^n}$$

This formula simply means that you discount each cash flow separately. Notice that the formula changes depending on the period, that is if you have to discount two periods (e.g., a year) you rise (1+r) to the power of 2.

---

35 The value of future cash flows has to be discounted due to the principle of "time value of money," which means that money in the present is worth more than money in the future due to inflation and the fact that if you dispose of it now, you can invest it.

This is because the rate is *compounded*, and this means that the money you receive in period two is discounted twice. You discount it once for period one, and then the remaining amount has to be discounted for period zero (present period). If the period you are using is "years," then you have to use an annual discount rate. The discount rate may be the expected return for your best alternative with a similar level of risk, or you can use the cost of borrowing money, which you can also define also as *weighted average cost of capital* (WACC).

The same formula of the NPV can be adjusted to calculate the *internal rate of return* (IRR). It calculates the "discount" that produces zero NPV. You will choose the project with the higher IRR.

Suppose you have two projects with similar ROI and NPV, but in the first one, you have a negative margin for the first four out of five years of the project, while in the second one you will *break even* at the end of the second year. This calculation is known as the "payback period"; it is the period it takes for your accumulated discounted cash flows to become positive. In fact, to break even means that accumulated revenue exceeds accumulated costs and you start producing profits.

Strategic Approach to Data Analysis

A data analyst not only has to be able to decide which type of analysis to perform, but also has to think strategically about what is worth spending time on. Thanks to his or her business acumen, the data analyst can define a data strategy[36] or analytics strategy. In the definition of this strategy, the data analyst has to adopt the broadest possible view, considering the needs of different areas, departments, and people, as well as the global view of the whole company since analytics directly affect its competitiveness.

The first step is to understand the company's strategy. You can start by filling the business model canvas presented earlier in this chapter. It is really important to understand the value proposition of your company, its raison d'être, and its goals. It is advisable to collect and organize this information either by getting existing documentation or by talking with people who have a strategic view of the company. Each department will have some specific needs, but sometimes they may not be so explicit, so you will have to understand and formulate strategic needs by yourself. In defining them, remember that you can help both the company as a whole and each department in two ways: to make better decisions or to improve operations.

In my previous book, *80 Fundamental Models for Business Analysts*, I explained several strategic models you can use to understand your company's strategy. Some of them are:

- Environmental Analysis (PEST): It identifies the key trends in the external environment (Political, Economic, Sociocultural, and Technological) that has and will have an impact on the company.
- Porter's Five Forces: It identifies the main actors of the competitive environment and the strength of your company in this environment.

---

36 Bernard Marr, *Data Strategy: How to Profit From a World of Big Data, Analytics and the Internet of Things* (London: Kogan Page, 2017).

- Competitive Map: It analyzes the positioning of your company versus that of its competitors in several items (price, service, quality, brand, etc.).
- VMOST: It identifies the Vision, Mission, Objectives, Strategies, and Tactics of your company.
- Product lifecycle analysis: The needs of your company depend also on the level of maturity of their products or services and this model helps identify in which maturity phase your company is.
- SWOT Analysis: It gathers all the information about the previous models to identify strengths, weaknesses, opportunities, and threats for your company.

There are three main levels on which the goals you established will have an impact: company, departments, and individuals. Since your main goals are the company's strategic objectives, they are defined at the company level but you will have to undertake a top-down process to align them with the different departments and, if feasible, with individuals (depending on the size and structure of the company). For example, if your goal is to increase the retention of customers, your customer service department will use analytics to improve retention incentives and customers' service, while your marketing department will need information about which kind of potential customers are more likely to become recurrent customers. Since the strategy may have several goals, you can use a double-entry matrix where in the first column you have all the key goals, and on the first row, you have all the areas of the company. In this matrix, you identify which areas are going to be impacted by which analytical goal and how.

	Sales	Marketing	Production	...
Revenues optimization				
Cross-selling				
Customers' satisfaction				
...				

Figure 13: Data strategy matrix

However, this top-down process is not the only one. Departments and even individuals have their specific requests. Listen to their needs and establish a bottom-up process where individual and departmental objectives are aligned with company goals. If some of the objectives are not aligned, you may modify them to be aligned, or perhaps you missed a company's goal that you can add to the analytics strategy.

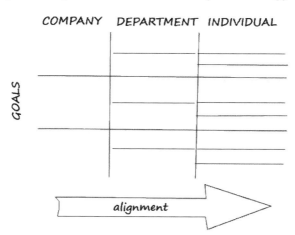

Figure 14: Goals alignment matrix

In figure 14, you can visualize all the aligned goals and now it's time to complement each of them with a KPI (a key performance indicator that measures the attainment of the goals) and, as far as practicable, the improvement you expect. Kaplan and Norton[37] call this improvement the "gap" to be closed. Using the previous example of improving retention incentives, your KPI could be the percentage of returning customers within a specific time frame, and your gap could be the difference between the actual retention rate and the desired retention rate.

To make the expected improvements in reality, you have to plan and execute several actions such as the creation of dashboards, reports, forecasts, and so forth. Actions must be tied to specific goals, and to facilitate this process start by transforming each goal into one or more strategic questions. If your goal is to increase customers' retention, one of your strategic questions may be "What are the reasons why customers switch to competitors?" or "Does a discount on the next purchase increase customers' retention?" Actions will follow as the answer to those questions. When I define possible actions, I find it useful to visualize them according to two variables:

- Type of analysis: descriptive/diagnostic, predictive, or prescriptive
- Timing: continuous (e.g., a sales dashboard), periodic, or ad hoc

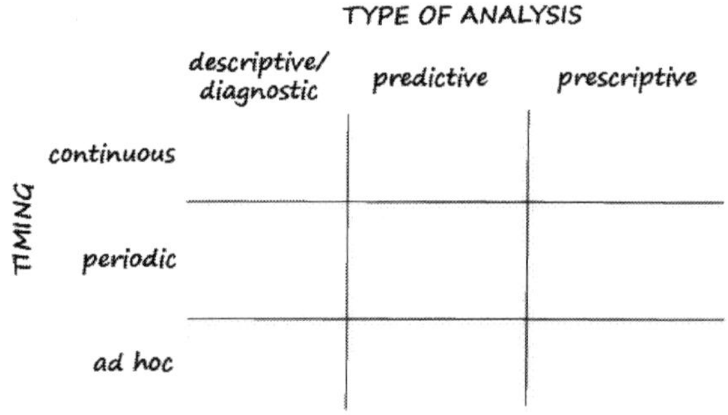

Figure 15: Matrix type of analysis/timing

---

37   Robert S. Kaplan and David P. Norton, *Execution Premium: Linking Strategy to Operations for Competitive Advantage* (Boston, MA: Harvard Business Press, 2009).

At this point, you'll probably realize that it may be difficult to establish specific strategic questions, above all for continuous actions with descriptive analytics, namely a dashboard. Keep in mind that instead of generating answers to specific questions, these kinds of actions pave the way to identify possible strategic questions.

For each action, you may create a canvas on the style of the Hypothesis Development Canvas developed by William Schmarzo.[38] Here I only suggest a simpler action-oriented matrix that allows to simply identify the main sub-actions.

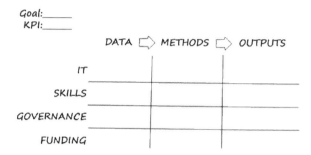

Figure 16: Action-oriented matrix

There are three main elements in a data analytics action:

- Data: Identify the different data sources and understand the meaning and kind of data they provide. The data you need depends on the method you are going to use to produce the expected output. If data for the chosen method is not available and can't be obtained, you should change the defined method, and, in certain cases, even your expected output. Data structure (structured, semistructured, and unstructured) and frequency (real-time, daily, weekly, etc.) are two important concepts when defining data sources.

---

38   https://www.kdnuggets.com/2018/11/data-science-activities-business-initiatives-hypothesis-development-canvas.html

- Methods: Methods depends on the kind of output and the kind of input you expect. The method or methods you will use are ways of simplifying and model real-world systems in order to make them more understandable and to help make better decisions. This is very important to remember before making any decision based on the results of these methods. Besides the use of ad hoc methods, in your data strategy, you should also define those processes that are going to be regularly repeated (i.e., the development of a model that estimates customers' lifetime value).
- Output: The output is about how you are going to exploit the information and knowledge produced by the action. Examples are dashboards, written reports, presentations, a specific answer to a question, etc.

To develop each action throughout the three elements (data, methods, and outputs), you need several enabling factors, or resources: IT, human resources, funding, and governance.

First, you need the technological resources to manage data, perform analytical methods, and present the results:[39]

- Data integration: Data has to pass from data sources to specifically structured the company's databases.
- Data grid: It includes all the elements that allow the storage and availability of data (data warehouses, data marts, aggregate DB, Hadoop, in-memory, etc.).
- Compute grid: The system that allows computation and data processing.
- Usage: Tools for reporting, business intelligence, data discovery, data visualization, etc.
- When evaluating different IT solutions, remember to take into consideration both the technical needs (tools that facilitate data

---

39   Rashed Haq, "Data Analytics: Creating a Roadmap for Success," *CROSSINGS: The Sapient Journal of Trading & Risk Management* (2014).

extraction, integration, processing, etc.) and the final users' needs. Usage tools must be user-friendly and provide enough analytical depth and flexibility. You may build the most solid architecture from the technical point of view, but if users face a difficult learning curve or if they need to rely on the IT department for minor changes, they will not use these tools. It means that the whole investment is worth nothing.

To implement and maintain an analytics strategy, you need people with specific *skills.* While the data strategy should be led by a business-oriented and creative person (namely the data artist), you will need different specialists, mainly IT people and statisticians. These people may be part of different departments, and you must be sure you have the necessary human resources. Then you need to establish how you will fund it (if necessary), and you have to clearly define roles and responsibilities (governance). However, skills, funding, and governance are beyond the scope of this book and I will let you explore the vast amount of resources available on this subject.

You may have realized at this point that several tasks (sub-actions) are common among the defined actions, for example, the creation of a Business Intelligence System is a common task among many actions (as the base for the creation of different dashboards, or the data source for specific studies and visualizations). Before establishing priorities, reorganize all the tasks to avoid redundancies. Use a double-entry table where on one side you have the tasks organized into categories and on the other side you have goals. Organizing tasks into categories facilitates the detection of common ones and possible synergies among them.

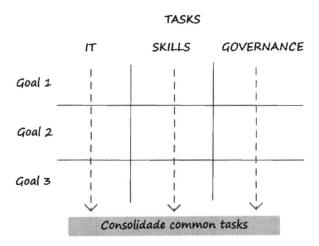

Figure 17: Tasks consolidation matrix

The next step is to establish priorities of your actions by defining for each priority the strategic relevance, expected benefits, costs, and possible risks. You can also establish a priority ranking of sub-actions based on the priorities of the related main actions. For each sub-action, define the percentage of accomplishment they represent for each action,[40] which helps you calculate their priority in the following way:

$$\sum_{i=1}^{n} Pr_i * Acc_j$$

Where i is a specific action, j is a specific sub-action, Pr is the priority of an action, and Acc is the percentage of accomplishment the sub-action represents for the related action. The priority is a number where the lowest value represents the lowest priority. In other words, the priority of a sub-action depends on its importance in accomplishing the actions, and the priority of these actions. This is a way to calculate the weighted average priority of sub-actions, but this may not be the optimal one

---

40   For example, the sub-action "creation of Business Intelligence System" represents the 40% in the accomplishment of the main action "creation of a dashboard."

depending on the circumstances. For example, you may choose to first execute the sub-actions of the most important action, then the sub-actions of the second most important actions, and so on.

Finally, it is beyond the scope of this book to cover market research and project management. However, the data artist should understand the basic concepts of market research in order to undertake or supervise some studies or when new data is needed. Concerning project management, it can be quite useful to apply the main principles when planning the data analytics strategy and all its actions and tasks. If you are interested in them, I suggest you start with the book *Strategic Approach to Market Research* by Anne E. Beall and *Project Management Lite* by Juana Clark Craig. In box 9, you can find the main concepts of market research, while in box 10 the main concepts of project management..

Box 9: Strategic Approach to Market Research

Sometimes you don't have the data you need to answer a specific question and you have to undertake market research to obtain it. Anne E. Beall[41] suggests taking a strategic approach to market research to avoid wasting time and money with useless studies. Figure 18 shows the five phases of the strategic approach to market research.

Figure 18: Strategic market research process (Source: Anne E. Beall, Strategic Market Research)

The first step is to define the overall objective and the main strategic questions of your research. In defining these questions, avoid listing too many small questions since they prevent the study from reaching

---

41   Anne E. Beall, *Strategic Market Research: A Guide to Conducting Research That Drives Businesses* (Bloomington, IN: IUniverse, 2010).

the sufficient depth to get actionable recommendations. On the other side, the few (or one) questions you define must be specific, measurable, and the answers to them must lead you to achieve the strategic objective you had identified. Taking the suggestions of Beall, an example of a poor question is "What do customers think about this potential new product?" while a better question would be "How likely would customers be to purchase this product with these specific features at this particular price?" From the main question(s), you derive several sub-questions whose responses will answer the main question.

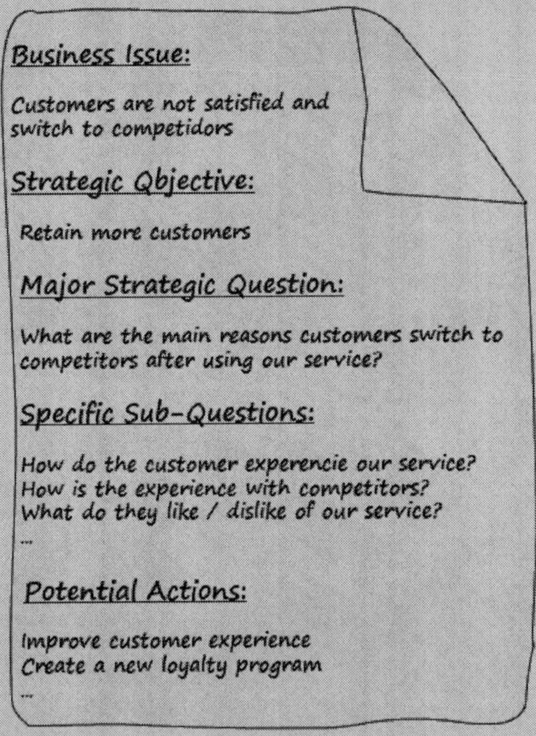

Figure 19: First step of strategic market research (Source: Anne E. Beall, Strategic Market Research)

The second step is to use hypotheses to better define the overall objective and guide the entire research. Using the example in the previous figure, a hypothesis may be that "price is the main reason for our high churn rate." It is important not to limit the research to simply answer the hypothesis, but you have to go deeper. For example, if it is not the price, what else is causing this churn rate? If it is the price, what price would they consider acceptable?

The third step is to choose the right method. First, decide whether to undertake qualitative or quantitative research. As a general rule, if there is not much research on the topic and you need a broad understanding of the subject, use qualitative methods; however if there is not much research but you need numbers to make a decision, first use a qualitative method to define the main issues and understanding on a subject, and then a quantitative method to obtain the numbers. In case there is extensive research on the subject, if you need a greater understanding, use a qualitative method, but if you need numbers, use a quantitative method.

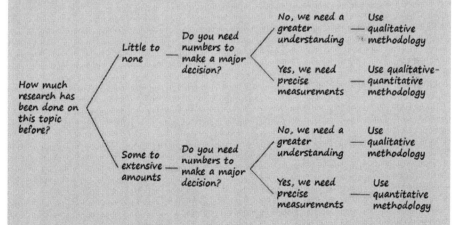

Figure 20: Decision tree to decide between qualitative vs. quantitative research (Source: Anne E. Beall, Strategic Market Research)

Box 10: Project Management

There are many books, courses, and available information about project management and it can get quite challenging to decide where to start. I don't consider myself an expert on project management but I strongly believe that knowing its main concepts has helped me tremendously to successfully carry out personal and professional projects.

There's a great book by Juana Clark Craig called *Project Management Lite* which explains in *plain English* the basic principles of project management, "just enough to get the job done. Nothing more."[42] I think this is perfect for data analysts since the majority of the projects are small to medium size and they are usually not very complex from a managerial point of view. In the next paragraphs, I'm going to describe the main concepts, but I sincerely suggest you read the book.

The purpose of project management is to help you do what you planned to do. To successfully achieve that, you should focus on three things:

- • - Clearly define the project and the plan.
- • - Work on the plan until it is done.
- • - Close the project.

Plan the Project
Step 1: Define What You're Trying to Do

First, you have to meet with your project *sponsor*, the person who commissioned the project. The conversation you have should help you end up with a clear understanding of:

- • Goals/outcome that must be SMARTER—Specific, Measurable, Agreed upon, Realistic, Time-bound, Ethical, and Resourced

---

42   Juana Clark Craig, *Project Management Lite: Just Enough to Get the Job Done ... Nothing More* (North Charleston, SC: CreateSpace, 2012).

- The reason why the project is important
- Critical constraints: people availability, time, money
- Budget: estimate it by thinking about the resources you need (people, external suppliers, facilities, tools)
- Minimum characteristics and things that must be done in order to consider the project successful
- Key events (*Milestones*), such as the start, when deliverables are due, when something important has to be accomplished before a new task could start, etc.
- What can go wrong (*Risks*)
- Who are the *stakeholders*, namely all the people affected by the project, from direct collaborators to people who may be affected by it? Think about how the project impacts them and how they may react. Also identify who needs to be informed as well as about what, when, how often, and how.

In analytical projects, this part is usually referred to finding the appropriate "business question" that deserves to be answered. To find the right question, first understand what are the levers that drive your business, who your customers are, and what they need. The adequate question is the one whose answer will be able to create a relevant positive impact on your organization.

After defining these concepts, fill in the possible gaps, and write them down in a *project charter*, which is the document that defines what you are going to do. Then also write the *plan* (step 2), that is the document that defines how you are going to do it. Don't forget to obtain the sponsor's approval on these documents before starting the projects.

Project Name:
Project Manager:
Sponsor:
Customer:

START: FINISH:

Budget:
Known Critical Constraints: Time, Money, and People
Reason for the Project: Why are we doing this?
Project Goal: What's the goal of the project / the expected outcome?
Scope: What are the requirements? What absolutely must be included?
What's considered done?: How will we know when we're done?

Key Milestones/Deliverable
Milestone | Deliverable | Due Date

Known Risks
What could go wrong | Chances | Impact | What should be done

Team
Role | Name | When needed | For how long

Communication Plan:
Who needs to know? What? Why? How often? How info is shared?

Figure 21: Project charter (Source: Adapted from
Juana Clark Craig, Project Management Lite)

Step 2: Come Up With a Plan to Do It

Take your project charter and start by your milestones and deliverables. Define what you need to accomplish them. If you have no experience of a certain kind of project, ask more experienced people, plan a brainstorming, or use mind maps (explored in the chapter "Be Creative"). When you have defined the tasks, resources, time, and people in charge needed to reach each milestone and deliverable, you have to schedule all of this. Organize it logically taking into account the tasks that can be done simultaneously and the tasks that depend on the accomplishments of previous ones (*dependencies*). Be careful to distinguish between time and duration. The first one is the effort needed to accomplish a task, while the second one is the length of the task or project. For example, if a task needs four hours to be completed, but the person in charge is only available one hour per day, then your duration will be at least four days. If you need a team for the project, it's a good practice to schedule a session where the whole team helps in the definition of the plan. You can use a whiteboard with sticky notes and markers to make the process more flexible and entertaining.

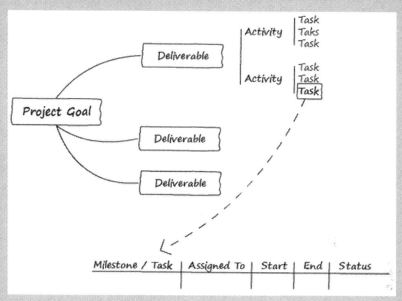

Figure 22: Project plan (Source: Adapted from Juana Clark Craig, Project Management Lite)

In analytical projects, plans usually include some standard phases: data collection and manipulation, choice of the analytical technique, generation of insights and recommendations.

Work on the plan
Step 3: Get Everyone Involved
Set an agenda for the kick-off meeting in which you will review the main characteristics of the project (see step 1). During the meeting,

use the agenda, the project charter, and the plan. Ensure you capture all relevant information that arises from it. During the kick-off meeting you should:

- Introduce the team.
- Review the project charter.
- Review the work plan.
- Review roles, responsibilities, and expectations.
- Review the reporting schedule and expectations.
- Review how problems and changes will be handled.
- Hold a Q&A.

Step 4: Make Sure the Work Gets Done
Hold regular review meetings if you are collaborating with a team or, if you are working alone, regularly check if you are on a schedule about the tasks, milestones, deliverables, time, and budget. If something has not been done, ask or verify the reason why and take measures to solve the problem.

Step 5: Handle the Problems
Track any problem that arises, define who is going to solve it, and identify the impacts it may have. Make sure no problem remains unsolved.

Step 6: Deal With Any Change
Track them, identify the implications, and if necessary, modify the project plan. Remember that if the plan changes significantly, you have to share this information with the sponsor.

Step 7: Manage the Team
If the project requires a team, you have to be a leader. Clearly define expectations, roles, and responsibilities. Moreover, you have to inspire them, keep things on track, organize regular meetings, take

responsibilities, help, keep the interest high, and welcome any suggestion. On the other hand, you too must expect skilled people, with experience, and who collaborate and participate actively.

Step 8: Keep Everyone Informed
This is very important in project management. Create a communication plan where you define when and what information has to be communicated. Write regular *status reports* where you describe the main accomplishments of the project as well as the problems and changes the project has suffered. Explain each delay, problem, or change. A good practice is to personalize the information since different stakeholders will need different pieces of information with a different schedule.

Close it out
Step 9: Wrap It Up
Hold a final project review (with the team) and ensure there are no important pending issues (deliverables, problems, etc.). Review that everything has been accomplished and delivered, check outstanding bills, revise the budget spend, and try to identify the lessons learned. Prepare a final status report and release the team.

In analytical projects, the presentation of the results is less about the project development and accomplishments, and much more about the insights and recommendations generated by the analysis. These must be presented in a concise, credible, and supported manner. In the section on data visualization ("Be a Designer"), we will discuss some practical suggestions to create good reports.

Step 10: Celebrate!

Understand the Human Mind

It is enough to read *Moneyball*[43] by Michael Lewis to understand the enormous improvement that the use of data and models can achieve compared to gut instinct. However, as the same author explains in *The Undoing Project*, such a model has its own limitations, which make it underperform compared to human judgment in certain cases. He tells the story of Daryl Morey who was using data and statistics to choose the best players for the NBA team Houston Rockets. Morey managed to improve the selection of NBA players but at a certain point, he understood he had reached the limits of the model. "The trick wasn't just to build a better model. It was to listen both to it and to the scouts at the same time. 'You have to figure out what the model is good and bad at, and what humans are good and bad at,' said Morey. Humans sometimes had access to information that the model did not, for instance."[44] However, if we are going to include human judgment in our models, we have first to understand its limitations, as we have done for data models. Lucky for us, in the seventies, Amos Tversky and Daniel Kahneman (Nobel laureate in Economics) started analyzing how people make decisions and their biases in judgment and choices. They stated that "these heuristics are highly economical and usually effective, but they lead to systematic and predictable errors."[45] The good news is that these heuristics (rules of thumbs and instinct) are usually good for decision making, and when they fail, errors tend to be systematic and predictable.

PREDICTABLY IRRATIONAL

Before explaining how people are "predictably irrational," you should know that the brain works using two systems.[46] System 1 works in an unconscious mode, is fast, and implies little effort since it reaches conclusions based on simple associations (including stereotypes). It is essential

---

43   Michael Lewis, *Moneyball: The Art of Winning an Unfair Game* (New York: W. W. Norton, 2003).

44   Michael Lewis, *The Undoing Project* (New York: Penguin, 2017).

45   Amos Tversky and Daniel Kahneman, "Judgment under Uncertainty: Heuristics and Biases," *Science* 185 (September 1974).

46   Daniel Kahneman, *Thinking, Fast and Slow* (New York: Penguin, 2012).

for our survival—if we had to reason about every decision, it would be very inefficient and exhausting. System 1 is responsible for reading emotions, remembering faces, using automatic skills (driving from home to work, eating), and so forth. It also helps us to take shortcuts for making decisions, for example when judging a person based on appearance or inferring that the quality of a bottle of wine is directly related to the price. System 2 is slower; it applies effort consciously and uses logic to reach conclusions. It is used when System 1 can't solve a situation due to the complexity of the task, for example, when you have to solve a math function or you have to drive along new roads. Despite the utopic idea of the "rational consumer," our brain is using System 1 85% of the time,[47] while the logical reasoning is made only when the intellectual task implies certain complexity or importance, for instance buying a house. However, even if System 2 tries to solve the situation with logic, it uses information from the associative memory of System 1. Therefore, even forcing ourselves to use System 2 won't be enough to avoid biased choices. These choices deviate from "rationality" for two broad reasons: (1) people's utility is not only monetary but also emotional; (2) in specific situations we misinterpret and misuse information.

Emotions play a crucial role in people's behavior and, therefore, in choices. Instead of utility, people try to maximize the pleasure from their emotional states, namely happiness and regret. For example, we value an object more if it is ours, due to the emotional attachment we feel. Its value is not merely economic, but it is the sum of monetary value and emotional value. Another example is the price we pay to avoid risk with insurances, even if the mere economic value of probabilities and outcomes suggests we are better off without insurances.

Besides our specific way of estimating utility, we tend to misinterpret and misuse information. Sometimes, data is incomplete because we only see things that happen and not things that don't happen, but we act as if we had access to complete information. When we apply a business

---

47   Martin Lindstrom, *Buyology: The New Science of Why We Buy* (New York: Doubleday, 2008).

strategy and it works, we see the choice as a success, but we can't compare it with the results of an alternative strategy. We not only perceive incomplete data as complete, but we also filter information in a biased way. We have a sort of confirmation bias according to which we tend to see what we expect to see. We like consistency with our beliefs; therefore, when we receive new information we accept it at once if it is in line with them, but we fiercely challenge it if it is not. Moreover, when we are faced with ambiguous information, we usually only see the aspects that agree with our beliefs. But the problem is not only biased filtering, but we also select the pieces of information and sources in a biased manner, that is, the ones closer to our thinking. For instance, when we try to prove something, if we find at once the information that confirms it, we stop our research, but if the information is not confirming it, we keep looking for new data. Problems don't end here though. Even when data is complete and we don't filter it, we can be biased by our interpretation of probability, statistics, and Bayesian inference.

We know mathematically how much 1% is, but our feeling of this probability for an event is higher than the actual probability. Would you prefer 200.000 € for sure or 99% chance to win 400.000 € and 1% chance of getting nothing? Are you in doubt about that? The first option has a weighted outcome of 200.000 €, while the second one has 396.000 €. I guess you are still in doubt about the choice you would make. On one side, it is because we place more weight on this 1% probability, and less weight on the 99%. On the other hand, in this situation, we also have risk aversion for the fear of disappointment if we finally receive nothing. This wouldn't be the case if we were offered this choice several times. This concept is useful for example in deciding the price gap of a refundable tariff versus a nonrefundable one (in airline tickets, hotel stays, etc.). Amos Tversky and Daniel Kahneman carried out a study where they estimated the weight people assign to probabilities (see figure 23). For small percentages, people tend to overweight probabilities due to what they called the "possibility effect." This explains why people play at lotteries. Progressing from something impossible (0%) to something improbable but possible (1%) is a huge increase in our minds. The opposite happens with higher probabilities, that is, people underestimate them.

Probability (%)	1	2	5	10	20	50	80	90	95	98	99	100
Decision weight	5.5	8.1	13.2	18.6	26.1	42.1	60.1	71.2	79.3	87.1	91.2	100

Figure 23: Probability vs. decision weight (Source: Adapted from Daniel Kahneman, Thinking, Fast and Slow)

The two authors crossed this information with the fact that we react differently to gains than to losses in a matrix called "the fourfold effect." This matrix explains situations such as lotteries or insurances where people make choices that would be considered "irrational" looking at the numbers.

	GAINS	LOSSES
HIGH PROBABILITY Certainty Effect	RISK AVERSE Accept an unfavorable settelment, i.e. accept €9.000 instead of 95% chance of getting €10.000	RISK SEEKING Reject favorable settelment, i.e. refuse to loose €9.000 and accept a 95% chance of loosing €10.000
LOW PROBABILITY Possibility Effect	RISK SEEKING Reject favorable settelment, i.e. buy a lottery ticket (pay €10 for the 0.0000001% possibility to win €1.000.000)	RISK AVERSE Accept an unfavorable settelment, i.e. accept to pay for an insurance (pay €100 inetead of accepting 0.1% chance of loosing €10.000)

Figure 24: The fourfold effect (Source: Adapted from Daniel Kahneman, Thinking, Fast and Slow)

Another misconception of probabilities is how we expect random events to appear. Have a look at the sex of six babies born in sequence at a hospital:[48]

---

48   This example is from *Thinking, Fast and Slow* (see Bibliography).

BBBGGG
GGGGG
BGBBGB

Do you think these sequences are equally likely? Even if you may think they are not, they are, as it is true for sequences of independent events with equal probabilities. This bias can make you identify patterns and causality where you just have random events, for example, two consecutive discount campaigns worked better than maintaining a higher price and you infer that this is a good choice for future strategies.

Related to probabilities and random events, we find the misuse of statistics. Daniel Kahneman presented a study made in the United States to decide in which school to invest. According to the results, the most successful schools, on average, were small. Therefore, huge investments were made to create smalls schools ignoring the fact that the variability of small schools was higher and that, probably, also the least successful schools, on average, were small. The problem is that we tend to substitute the use of sampling errors with finding an intuitive causal explanation for the results. In this story, it may seem reasonable that small schools perform better because of more personalized attention and encouragement to students. However, if results were the opposite, we could easily create another story saying that larger schools are better because of available resources, curricular offerings, and so forth.

While we misinterpret probabilities and statistics, sometimes we completely forget about Bayesian inference, that is, we ignore statistical base rates (or prior probabilities). For example, in evaluating the outcome of a promotional campaign we are launching, we tend to use close and specific information such as the content, the investment, the team who works on it, the feeling we have, and so forth and tend to ignore (or underestimate) prior probabilities, namely the average outcome of similar campaigns. Ignoring prior probabilities makes our estimations more extreme because of two factors:

- Substitution effect: An extreme evidence is translated into an extreme outcome without assessing the real impact. We may think that our campaign will have huge success because we invested double, but maybe the investment only contributes in a small percentage to its success.
- Overconfidence: We tend to be overconfident in the things we do, approximating estimations to the best-case scenario instead of the most probable scenario.

After this introduction about how our mind works, we will look at some of the main biases that affect judgment and how to overcome them.[49]

RECIPROCITY

This is a strong social need. We feel a strong desire to give back to those who give us something, despite the importance of what we received or whether or not we wanted it. When car dealers offer a coffee or when we are given a "free" gift, it is not mere altruism. It is based on the principle that the initial gift does not have to be proportionate to what we feel obliged to give back, that is, by purchasing what we have been offered. Not giving back makes us feel shame and a bad conscience. The gift doesn't have to be tangible; for instance, when we praise or improve someone's self-esteem, we create a sort of need for reciprocation. A similar effect is produced when we first refuse an important commitment, and then we feel obliged to commit to something smaller. For example, a boy scout asks us to donate $1,000 to an association and we feel ok by gently refusing to donate. The boy scout then asks us just to buy a box of cookies to help the association and we feel obliged to do it because of our first refusal.

---

49   These concepts come from different books: *Thinking, Fast and Slow*; *The Undoing Project*; *How We Know What Isn't So*; *Buyology*; *50 Psychology Classics*; *Influence*; *Blink*; *The Paradox of Choice*; *Predictably Irrational*; and *Brandwashed* (see the Bibliography).

CONSISTENCY

System 1 likes consistency and coherence, and hates incongruent, contradictory, and vague things. This has an impact on two issues. On one side, we want to be consistent with our principles, beliefs, and attitudes by behaving in line with them, even if some new circumstances make this choice not optimal. On the other side, we distort the information we receive to make it consistent with the entire story or our beliefs (Hindsight bias). However, when there is an evident dissonance between attitude and behavior, our brain tries to go back as soon as possible to our comfort zone by reframing our attitudes, by modifying our behavior, or by looking for additional information to solve the dissonance. This is why good marketers don't try to change your attitudes, but they aim at influencing your behavior with facts. Money-back guarantees exploit this principle (but not only this one) to modify your behavior without trying to change your attitude. You may still think that this new generation TV is not worth the extra price, but since you can give it back without losing anything, you are not contradicting your attitude. Finally, if you keep it, the dissonance will make you gradually modify your attitude or to find some explanations that justify the contradiction (i.e., "I wanted to give it back but my kids loved it so I kept it for them . . .").

COMMITMENT

Related to consistency, commitment is another strong motivation for our brain. If we commit to something, we feel socially and morally obligated to our choice, even if—given the new circumstances—we wouldn't have taken the same decision. Suppose you commit to help a friend in organizing a party. In the beginning, the party was supposed to be just for a dozen people, but finally, your friend invites fifty people. This would imply much more work for you, but because you have already committed to it, it is quite difficult to withdraw. This feeling is strengthened if you had already started to help or if you feel very involved in the organization. This is similar to when you are convinced by a seller to enter his or her shop or when someone asks your opinion, you are more easily persuaded. The commitment is stronger when it involves social norms (helping a friend) than with market norms (being compensated with money). For example, if you had committed to help in exchange for money, in the new situation it would have been less difficult to refuse to help or to ask for more money.

SOCIAL PROOF

Unless we are strongly sure about what to do, we tend to look for social approval before we act. Take, for example, the famous story of Catherine Genovese who was murdered in the middle of a crowded street in New York after having been attacked several times. This story proved that due to the ambiguity of the situation, nobody acted because nobody else did it, everybody considered appropriate not to act because other people were not doing anything. Today, the widespread use of social media has magnified the need for social proof, which is probably one of the main drivers in influencing people's behavior. This principle is also used when you have background laughter in comedy shows. It is also valid when we decide to buy something since other people are buying it. Therefore, sometimes, it compensates to give something for free in the beginning to foster the herd behavior.[50]

LIKING

If people are like us, we tend to like them more and have a better (and probably biased) opinion of them. The opposite is also true. This is also referred to as the "halo effect," and this is the reason why celebrities are so apt for product testimonials. In addition, the "lure of celebrities" is also explained by the fact that we all want to emulate our idols or become like them.

AUTHORITY

People have a natural tendency to listen to those in charge, with titles, with uniforms, or who show signs of success (i.e., having an expensive

---

50   *Herd behavior* describes how members of a group act similarly without someone leading them.

car). We unconsciously give them a sort of authority on us, which may or may not be real.

SCARCITY

The more difficult it is to obtain something, the more appealing it becomes. Expiration dates and limited editions are artificial elements that create scarcity to increase the perceived value of something. This is related to "loss aversion," for example, concerning choices. We prefer to increase our possible choices or maintain the ones we have. However, this leads to the "paradox of choice" since even if we have more choices that make us happier, with more options we have more responsibility, a higher probability to make a mistake, and overall dissatisfaction with the final choice.

REPRESENTATIVENESS

We associate and judge things based on similarity, but sometimes the similarity we evaluate has nothing to do with what we have to judge. For example, we tend to make inferences based on the aspect of people (their job, character, etc.). These are typical stereotypes that we apply to a range of different things and the problem arises when we use superficial characteristics to infer more profound ones. A strategy doesn't have to work just because it worked in the past, or a product doesn't have to be successful just because it belongs to a company we all love. When the question is too complex, we tend to answer a simpler question (instead of "Will this product be successful?" we answer the question "Do we like this product?").

AVAILABILITY

We tend to remember only the most remarkable and/or most recent events, and we think they are more likely to happen. It is a common "misbelief" that infertile couples that adopt are more likely to have a child afterward thanks to being less obsessed with conceiving.[51] This has been

---

51   Thomas Gilovich, *How We Know What Isn't So: Fallibility of Human Reason in Everyday Life* (New York: The Free Press, 1993).

disproved and the reason for this popular belief is that people tend to talk about and remember only remarkable events. In general, people tend to remember things that they observe themselves more easily than the things they heard about, as well as vivid events such as lottery wins, catastrophes, and so forth.

HINDSIGHT BIAS

We like to rationalize events and give meaning to them. We like to see order, meaning, and patterns even when they don't exist. This generates the "hindsight bias" when, after a certain event occurs, they are perceived far more predictable than they were. This occurs for example when historians describe the outcomes of battles, or commentators describe the result of a match. The problem is that we seldom remember our forecast before the event, or it was so ambiguous that it can be adapted to the result. This generates overconfidence and can undermine the correct prediction of future events.

FRAMING

Several studies have shown that the framing of available options can change our decisions;[52] since framing modifies our perception of value, we can exploit different biases and change the framing to obtain a different choice:

- Perceived value of losses is greater than perceived value of gains; you should convince someone to invest in your business not by listing the possible gains but by highlighting the opportunity loss it implies if one does not invest in it.
- Perceived variations in value decrease with the increase of the amount of reference (e.g., the perceived value between € 10 and € 20 is greater than between € 110 and € 120, even if the amount we lose or gain is the same, € 10).

52   Amos Tversky and Daniel Kahneman, "The Framing of Decisions and the Psychology of Choice," *Behavioral Decision Making* (1985): 25–41.

- We tend to take into account sunk costs, even if to take the optimal rational decision we shouldn't. Suppose you spent time, energy, and money on a project that is going to fail. However, there is only a minimal chance you can save it if you invest a couple of weeks more. In this case, if you were rational, you would just consider the improbable gain and the extra effort needed, without considering what you have already done.

LAW OF SMALL NUMBERS

System 1 is not very good at calculating probabilities. We know that if we toss a coin, we have a 50% chance of heads and a 50% chance of tails. However, we can have proof of it when we toss the coin many times. If we toss it twice, we forget that the second toss has a 50% probability of getting the same result as the first one, and a 50% probability of getting the opposite result. People also apply this bias to more complex situations, forgetting that there is no "law of small numbers."

REGRESSION TO THE MEAN

People don't use this principle when evaluating events or results. After a very good or very bad result, it is more likely to have something less extreme. This applies for instance to companies' performance in consecutive years or students' grades. Daniel Kahneman narrates a story about how in the Israeli Air Force, instructors thought that praising a flight cadet's good performance produced bad results, whereas punishing him or her produced better results. Even if these facts were true, it wasn't the reward or punishment that affected performance, but the regression to the mean. Extraordinary good performances tend to be followed by a lower one, while very bad ones tend to be followed by something better. This is important when we, as analysts, have to make predictions with not much information. Let's say you have to estimate the sales of different stores for the following year knowing that the overall sales for that year are estimated to increase by 10%. You may be tempted to assign better-than-average performance to the stores that most sold this year or assign 10% to all of them. However, if there is no specific explanation for that, you should follow the principle of regression to the mean and give a better result to those who underperformed this year.

ANCHORING

When we are doubtful about something, we tend to stick to the first information we hear. Suppose you have to negotiate the price of a project with a consultancy but you have no idea about the possible price. The consultant gives you a certain price in the beginning and you unconsciously think that the approximate value is that one, even if you may think it is too high, or you may think the consultant can inflate it. This works in many other situations when we have no clear reference point. In some cases, anchoring is arbitrary and the reference point may not even be related to the new situation. Experiments have shown that using arbitrary numbers as reference points for product prices affects the respondents' willingness to pay.[53]

HALO EFFECT

This is the effect of the first impression that is maintained and projected. In a job interview, if the first impression of the candidate is good, the rest will seem better. During a holiday, if the first impression when entering the hotel is unpleasant (for example, we are made to wait for the room) all the other facilities and services will seem worse. This is caused by our need to reach some conclusions with the available information (first impression) and the need to be consistent with our beliefs. Evaluating different elements separately helps reducing this bias.

OWNERSHIP (ENDOWMENT EFFECT)

We tend to overestimate the value of what we own, for example, when we want to sell a house to which we are emotionally attached or when we want to sell something that we gained with difficulty. This effect is related to the general loss aversion we feel, and it is exploited with money-back guarantees, free trials, and so forth—that is, when we own something

---

53   Dan Ariely, *Predictably Irrational: The Hidden Forces That Shape Our Decisions* (New York: Harper Perennial, 2010).

even for a small period of time and then we are faced with the possibility to lose it.

RELATIVITY

This is related to framing, since we tend to value an option differently if compared to new elements. It is also related to the reference point, since the appearance of new elements changes it. For example,[52] the magazine *The Economist* was offering three options: online-only subscription for $59; print-only for $125; and online and print for $125. Objectively, the second option is useless, since the third one costs the same and offers something more. However, it has an important function—to give you a context, a reference point, on the value of the subscription. You may not be sure whether the cheaper online subscription or a more expensive print one is better for you, but you may have the perception that with the third option you are obtaining the online version for free. This strategy moves more choices from the online-only to the paid and online option.

EMOTIONS

Emotions alter decision-making; it is better to avoid making decisions when we are excited or upset. Positive emotions make us more positive, while negative ones have the opposite effect. Arousal effect on sales is not a stereotype; it actually exists. Fear is probably one of the emotions that has the strongest effect. In fact, products that alleviate the fear of falling ill, becoming fat, being robbed, etc. have a strong persuasive power.

EXPECTATIONS

The "placebo effect" is based on the impact of expectations on mind and body, for example when patients who receive sugar pills feel improvements on their illness. Strong expectations on certain results affect the results themselves. This is why it is important to present well a product since the expectation it generates at the beginning will affect positively or negatively the experience. However, if expectations are too high, then this effect won't work and it will produce the disappointment.

BALANCE

The most persuading element is combining the heuristic/emotional part with the logic part. When the other person feels that what you are saying is also backed up by logic, you are more convincing. It also works if you provide a little logic in your explanation. Studies have shown that simply including the word "because" increases the persuading power even if the subordinate clause doesn't have a strong or pertinent logic.[54]

HOW TO OVERCOME BIASES

The first step to overcome biases is to understand them, this has been the purpose of describing them thus fare. In addition, there are some useful recommendations you can follow:

- Force your mind to think differently, for example, by accepting different points of view, openly evaluating news that contradicts your beliefs, and trying to go beyond superficial aspects.
- Whenever you can, use data, measure, and apply statistics; to avoid the "law of small numbers," use sampling error calculations to evaluate results.
- Be scrupulous in using control groups and random sampling in your analyses.
- Precisely define outcomes and estimates in advance; when an outcome occurs, analyze and register the feedback.
- Predict different scenarios instead of just one and assign them probabilities; this will help you avoid being overconfident and predicting just the best-case scenario; if you only have positive scenarios, hypothetically imagine that the outcome is negative and write down why it has happened.
- Don't include sunk costs in your decisions.

---

54   Kahneman, *Thinking.*

- Include prior probabilities to avoid extreme estimations.
- Instead of judging the whole of something (e.g., a candidate for a job), judge different attributes separately and use simple statistics for the final decision.

Go Beyond Statistics

Relying on analytics instead of just gut instinct can boost the competitive advantage of companies.[55] In a competitive environment where companies sell similar products, use similar technologies, and similar marketing strategies, implementing a sound analytical strategy means creating a difficult-to-reply competitive advantage. This is the actual mainstream point of view concerning analytics, according to which quantitative analyses through technology represent the victory of objectivity over subjectivity in decision-making. Objectively, relying more on data and statistics can enormously improve decision-making. Read *Moneyball* and you'll grasp their immense potential. However, even if this trend is well justified, it has had a detrimental effect on the reputation of human intuition and humanities. This is why we are hearing greater voices reclaiming the importance of humanities and qualitative analysis.

Christian Madsbjerg explains in his book *Sensemaking*[56] that algorithms cannot explain human nature, since it is based on uncertainty, ambiguity, conflicting information, and context. To really understand human nature, you have to develop your abilities based on humanities such as anthropology, psychology, art, history, and so forth. The author preaches the superiority of humanities offers interesting examples of top CEOs with degrees in humanities. To really understand the truth, you must go beyond abstract data and use "sensemaking," because while algorithms can go wide analyzing billions of abstract data, sensemaking goes deep into real meaning.

Madsbjerg makes a great point in his book; however, there are important limits to relying only on sensemaking. First, decisions based on qualitative results can be biased by the researcher's human nature itself. In some cases, numbers can help researchers reduce these biases. Secondly, applying sensemaking on a large scale is practically impossible due to cost and time constraints, while automated algorithms are extremely cost- and time-efficient, even if the analysis can't go too deep.

---

55   Thomas H. Davenport and Jeanne G. Harris, *Competing on Analytics: The New Science of Winning* (Boston, MA: Harvard Business School Press, 2007).
56   Christian Madsbjerg, *Sensemaking: The Power of the Humanities in the Age of the Algorithm* (New York: Hachette Books, 2017).

I think the key is to understand the limits of both approaches and not only make them complement each other but also use them to reach a superior level of analytics. For example, a deep anthropological and psychological understanding of certain consumer behavior can help improve the algorithm that analyzes facial expressions captured through cameras.

To reach a great analytical level, the data artist needs to master not only conventional analytical skills (math, statistics, etc.) but also unconventional abilities.[57] This chapter will focus on these kinds of abilities, namely those that can push the data analyst beyond the conventional quantitative analysis. In addition, it is extremely important for the analyst to know in which circumstances one type of analysis should be preferred to a different one. The matrix in figure 25 has been created for facilitating the analytical process, but it is far from being exhaustive or scientifically proven. Moreover, the boundaries between the categories are not clear lines; they are quite blurred, and many data analyses are mixed and include more than one method. For example, you can use prior probability (deductive quantitative data analysis) to improve statistical analysis such as forecasts (inductive quantitative data analysis), or you can use the results of in-depth interviews (inductive qualitative data analysis) to define the questions of an online survey (inductive quantitative data analysis). The key is to understand which method works better in which circumstances and to understand their limits. With this information, you'll be also able to create the best "blended" model for each situation.

---

57   Despite the emphasis on nontechnical skills, the data artist must be a numerate person, comfortable with math, and have a good background in statistics. He or she doesn't have to be able to develop machine-learning algorithms or apply other complex statistical methods, but should be able to perform basic statistical analysis such as hypothesis testing, correlations, regressions, cluster analysis, classification analysis, and factor analysis with the help of proper analytical tools. He or she needs to be able to apply those methods in the right situations and know the limitations of each. If you are a statistician or an analyst with a strong numerical background, you are certainly mastering these topics; otherwise you will have to develop these skills first. If you are not familiar with statistics or you have scant knowledge, I would start with *Naked Statistics* and *How Not to Be Wrong* (see Bibliography).

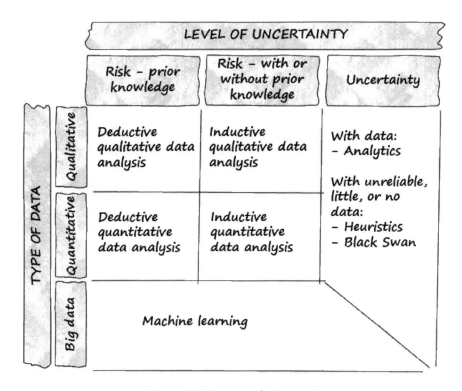

Figure 25: Data analysis matrix

On one hand, the type of analysis depends on the type of data (qualitative, quantitative, or big data). Qualitative data usually comes from qualitative market research methods and is recorded as text, pictures, videos, podcasts, and so forth. Quantitative data comes from either research methods such as surveys or from tools that keep track of business operations, customer interactions, and so forth. Big data concerns the availability of great volumes of data in structured and/or unstructured format (e.g., data from sensors).

On the other hand, the type of analysis depends on the level of uncertainty, namely our underlying knowledge and prior research on the topic. Mousavi and Gigerenzer[58] described three different processes in

58   Shabnam Mousavi and Gerd Gigerenzer, "Risk, Uncertainty, and Heuristics," *Journal of Business Research* 67, no. 8 (2014): 1671–78.

decision-making under risk and uncertainty. These processes are not exclusive—in other words, they can overlap in several situations. Under risk, you can use deductive analysis by applying prior probabilities to the problem. An example of deductive analysis is estimating the ROI of a campaign based on the average ROI of similar campaigns. This implies that we have some previous knowledge about the subject. Alternatively, under risk you can use inductive reasoning by applying statistical inference. Using the previous example, you would test the campaign with a sample of your customers and you infer the results to your entire customer base. Statistical inference doesn't need prior information but it has other requirements. Depending on the method, you may need a minimum of data and/or a certain data distribution and variability. In hypothesis testing, you must have a clear null hypothesis, namely the default answer that you would choose in case of not undertaking the analysis (e.g., "the campaign has not impact so I don't implement it"). This isn't necessarily something you believe to be true (as in the deductive analysis where you have prior beliefs based on prior knowledge), but it may represent the status quo or the action with the lower risk; for example, to increase prices only if you can prove that it won't impact customers' satisfaction. "[Statistical inference] is the science of changing your mind under uncertainty"[59] and not the science of giving you an answer from scratch; therefore, you must have a clear default answer or action in hypothesis testing. Think about it in statistical terms for a moment. Swapping the null hypothesis with the alternative hypothesis completely changes the meaning of the analysis and results can be the opposite. In fact, statistical inference does not prove something to be true; it does or does not disprove the null hypothesis. The null hypothesis is rejected if the resulting p value is lower than α (alpha), which is usually a small number: 0.05. Since α represents the error where we reject the null hypothesis despite being true, if you swap the hypotheses you are accepting a completely different error. In other words, you are wrongly framing your decision-making. To better explain

---

59   Cassie Kozyrkov, https://towardsdatascience.com/whats-the-point-of-statistics-8163635da56c

this concept, I borrow an example by Cassie Kozyrkov.[60] Suppose you have to explore a new planet and find out whether it is inhabited by aliens or not. To explore it, you have limited resources and you can only search a small portion of it, namely, you have to infer the presence of aliens by a small sample, just like in hypothesis testing you infer a characteristic of an entire population with a sample. At this point, the key is to establish your null hypothesis—the default action that you would undertake without any information about this planet. Imagine that the goal of the exploration is to establish a planet base to study alien life. What would you do in the absence of any information? It seems reasonable not to invest a huge amount of money to build a base, so your default action is "not to invest." Your null hypothesis is then "there is no alien life on the planet." To disprove the null hypothesis, you must find some proof that "makes it ridiculous," or, in statistical terms, you need your p value to be lower than the established alpha. In our example, finding an alien would disprove the null hypothesis and confirm that the alternative hypothesis is true: "there is alien life on the planet." Therefore, we would switch our action from not investing to investing in the planet base. On the contrary, if we don't find any alien, we can't reject the null hypothesis, but this does not mean we can say it is true. Not finding any alien on this small portion of the planet does not imply that the planet is not inhabited. Now imagine that you switch the hypotheses. Your null hypothesis is that there are aliens. To disprove that, you explore a small portion of the planet and find no form of life. Following the rules of statistical inference, you should reject that "there are aliens on the planet" and confirm that there is no alien on it. On the contrary, if you find an alien, you can't reject that it is inhabited, but you also can't confirm it. This may seem not very logical, but this is the result of not establishing a proper null hypothesis and default action before undertaking the test.

If you lack prior knowledge, the appropriate data for inferential statistics, or a default answer in hypothesis testing, then risk becomes uncertainty and it can't be dealt with statistics or probabilities. Under this level

---

60   https://hackernoon.com/statistical-inference-in-one-sentence-33a4683a6424

of uncertainty, you need a different approach: abductive reasoning. Philosophers may refer to it as the "inference to the best explanation,"[61] namely your "best guess" having neither previous information nor statistical proof. There are several methods you can use here. If you have some data at your disposal, use analytics. By analytics, I mean "exploratory data analysis" or "data mining" using tables, graphs, comparisons, evolutions, and so forth to identify a plausible answer. Analytics is also the best way to start if you don't have a clear question about the analysis. If you have no data (or too little) and/or it is unreliable (too much noise, errors, etc.), use heuristics or the Black Swan approach proposed by Nassim Nicholas Taleb, which I will explain later.

Finally, if you have at your disposal a huge amount of data in a constant stream (what you may know as big data), machine learning is probably the best option. This kind of analysis uses examples instead of instructions to give you an answer.[62] For instance, the more pictures of a dog you provide as examples, the more the algorithm will accurately recognize a new picture of a dog as a "dog."

61   Elliot Sober, *Core Questions in Philosophy: A Text With Readings*, 6th edition (Upper Saddle River, NJ: Pearson, 2012).
62   https://hackernoon.com/the-simplest-explanation-of-machine-learning-youll-ever-read-bebc0700047c

Qualitative Data Analysis

Compared to quantitative analysis, qualitative data analysis focuses on language instead of numbers, and usually, there are no established or fixed variables. It uses information from interviews, observations, descriptions, and so forth to describe the social experience focusing on the whole instead of the individual elements. For this reason, interactions and context are very important. Another clear difference with quantitative methods is that qualitative analysis usually starts during the very process of data collection, which is adapted on the way. For example, an ethnographer can make some interpretations during some observations and then try to prove these interpretations in the following observations.

Usually, qualitative data analysis allows you to go deeper into the topic you are studying and to better understand the "why." You may ask in an online survey to rate the likelihood of buying a new product and the results are positive, but finally, the sales are not at the level you expected. You decide to undertake a focus group or in-depth interviews and you discover that when you start asking more details, people are saying something like "It is a great product for that person, but for me . . ." or that they will buy it but in the future, and so forth. In this case, this may reveal that some doubts exist about the product and that a superficial answer won't reveal the actual behavior of potential customers. Moreover, actually observing people may reveal additional information that they are not saying. Anne E. Beall provides an example of a group of women who were testing some shampoos. While they said they would choose the product based on quality, the first thing they did on receiving the product was to smell it (so fragrance was quite important in their choice of shampoo).[63]

INDUCTIVE QUALITATIVE DATA ANALYSIS
It is beyond the purpose of this book to exhaustively explain the methods and techniques of qualitative data analysis, but I will give you a brief

---

63   Beall, *Strategic Market Research*.

overview of the process that you can use (the information is mainly based on the book *Investigating the Social World*[64]).

1. Conceptualization. During and after the process of data collection, the analyst starts interpreting the observations and deriving important concepts. These concepts are then tested in different or following observations, since the frequency of appearance denotes the importance and generalization of the concept. If a concept is consistently observed several times, an explanatory model can be defined. These concepts can be defined either based on previous studies or established theories, or they can be specific to the study.

2. Coding and Categorization. Interpretations and concepts are usually structured, categorizing them using a checklist matrix where the first column identifies the features that have to be observed. One or more columns are added to organize the information related to each feature. This matrix is also useful to represent a summary of the data collected.

FEATURES	on board	at the airport
stress		
behavior		
...		

Figure 26: Checklist matrix

3. Relationship Examination and Data Display. In this phase, you explore the relationship (or correlation) among concepts or different concept features by using a double-entry matrix. You can either observe the cases where two concepts appear together, or the cases where the presence of a specific feature of a concept appears together with a feature of a different concept. For example, during the analysis of customers'

---

64   Russell K. Schutt, *Investigating the Social World: The Process and Practice of Research* (Thousand Oaks, CA: Sage, 2019).

satisfaction, you create a matrix with three features (levels) of overall satisfaction (low, medium, high) on one side, and three features about the recommendation intention (improbable, probable, highly probable) on the other side. In each of the nine cells, you write the summary of a case or reporting quotes, as well as take note of the frequency (the number of observations where the two features were present). The use of template and frameworks (double-entry tables, flux diagrams, word clouds, etc.) is fundamental in order to identify patterns, anomalies, correlations, and so forth.

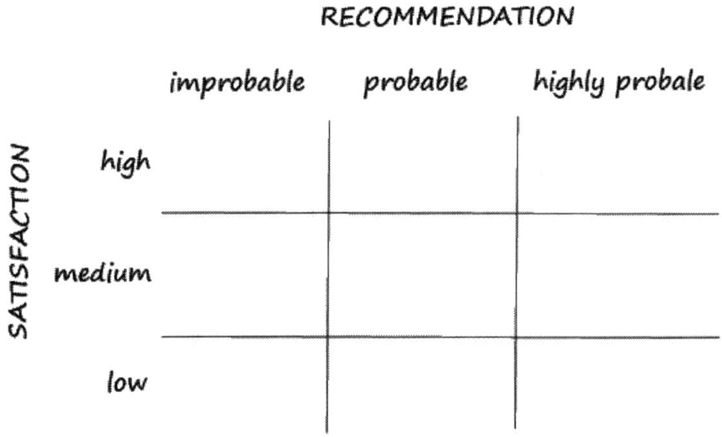

RECOMMENDATION

Figure 27: Coding matrix

If you have a certain number of observations and you use frequency in these matrices, you are "enumerating" your information. This means that instead of (or besides) using a classic subjective method, you use quantitative approaches used in statistics, namely non-parametric methods for hypothesis testing.[65] For example, you can use chi-square to test whether negative words are more often used by younger customers compared to older ones. The table in figure 28 demonstrates

---

65 Parametric methods for hypothesis testing require a certain number of observations and usually the normal distribution of data. Since qualitative data nálisis tends to have a limited number of observations, only non-parametric models are proposed in this section.

some of the non-parametric models that you can use and that I've described in my previous book *80 Fundamental Models for Business Analysts*. Enumeration can be used either to add information to traditional qualitative methods or to build a proper empirical study.

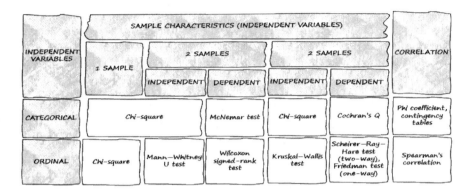

Figure 28: Non-parametric models (Source: Alberto Scappini, 80 Fundamental Models for Business Analysts)

4. Concluding. Finally, conclusions are derived from the analysis, paying particular attention to conclusion authentication. This means that the analyst has to revise and describe the credibility of the informant and the possible biases introduced by the situation and/or the analyst. It is a good practice to describe the whole process of data analysis since there is no specific or standard methodology as in statistical analysis. This description improves the confidence in the conclusions.

DEDUCTIVE QUALITATIVE DATA ANALYSIS

Deductive qualitative research is based on previous knowledge and theories that are tested during the study. You can use an analytical process similar to the one proposed for the Inductive Qualitative Data Analysis, with the difference that the variables and framework are defined by previous knowledge or specific theory. In deductive qualitative analyses, you are not discovering patterns or relations, but you are testing them versus a specific hypothesis.

As for the inductive approach, you can apply numeric methods by quantifying or "enumerating" prior information. For example,[66] imagine you are testing a disease and you don't have prior numeric probabilities

---

66   M. A. Medow and C. R. Lucey, "A Qualitative Approach to Bayes' Theorem," *Evidence-Based Medicine* 16, no. 6 (2011): 163–67.

but just qualitative information. You can define prior probabilities into discrete categories: very unlikely, unlikely, uncertain, likely, and very likely. In the case of being at the extremes (very unlikely and very likely), a test won't change the new probability of having the disease due to the Bayesian theorem. Therefore, unless you are dealing with a dangerous disease, a test may not be necessary. However, if you are in the intermediate categories, you may perform the test and decide that, for example, you move the final probability by one category (the direction depends on the result of the test, positive or negative).

SENSEMAKING

Sensemaking is a data analysis method introduced by Christian Madsbjerg and Mikkel B. Rasmussen that allows the analyst to go deeper into the meaning of things, instead of only taking a superficial approach on a large scale with pure quantitative analyses.

Context is very important in sensemaking. The meaning of something can't be considered in a vacuum, but it depends on the relation of it with other elements—that is, the meaning of this element is defined by the relation it has with the other elements. The importance of the context is visible also in simple analyses, for example, if you analyze the evolution of sales in a specific time frame, you should take into account many external elements: behavior of competitors, weather, seasonality, events, technical problems, and so forth. Another important concept is phenomenology, namely, the issue is how people experience life and the researcher has to discover the "why" instead of just focusing on visible facts. In addition to context, you have to remember that human behavior is "irrational" (as explained in the chapter "Understand the Human Mind") and depends on social relationships. Since sensemaking uses anthropology, psychology, sociology, art, and culture, it can help understand and predict human behavior better than pure quantitative analyses.

The process of sensemaking can be broken down into five steps:[67]

---

67   C. Madsbjerg and M. B. Rasmussen, "An anthropologist walks into a bar...," *Harvard Business Review* (March 2014); Christian Madsbjerg and Mikkel B. Rasmussen,

- Reframe the problem: I've already talked about this concept in the first part of this book (see Creative Techniques in the chapter "Be Creative"). Here, a problem should be reframed as a phenomenon, namely the human experience. Instead of asking "How can we reduce the churn rate of our magazine subscribers?" ask "How do our subscribers experience reading, and why they are leaving?" To properly reframe the problem, you must challenge the underlying assumptions, starting with the most general ones (people are rational, tomorrow will be similar to today, our hypotheses are unbiased . . .) to the most specific to your business.
- Collect the data: Several qualitative research methods are used in this phase, but the most insightful ones are observation and ethnography where the researcher can study people in their real "habitats." Data collection is designed specifically to challenge assumptions and hence it is executed without any preliminary hypothesis or preconception and is open-ended research.
- Look for patterns: For me, this is the most interesting element in sensemaking. While the type of data collection of sensemaking has already been widely used in market research (i.e., qualitative market research), you may be less familiar with the human sciences-based analysis. This analysis aims at discovering the hidden root causes, the "why" to human behavior. It starts with the most external layer of human experience represented by simple observable facts. Then it goes deeper to the intermediate layer where habits and practices make you understand the choices and behavior of people. And finally, the last layer contains the underlying causes of these choices and behavior. The search for patterns can be divided into three parts:
  o A general but sophisticated analysis of what it means to be a human being and life in a specific context.

The Moment of Clarity: Using the Human Sciences to Solve Your Hardest Business Problems (Boston, MA: Harvard Business Review Press, 2014).

o The use of specific human science theories to discover patterns (see box 11).

o Abductive reasoning: As already explained in the chapter "Be Creative," abductive reasoning allows reaching new ideas through the observation of incomplete evidence and the use of creative leaps, intuition, and imagination to identify the "why."

• Create key insights: Now that you have identified the underlying reasons for a certain behavior, you can reduce the gap between assumptions and the real experience. At this stage, you identify where to act to improve the situation. You change underlying assumptions such as "Our subscribers are leaving because we are expensive and they can find free news" with "They enjoy reading without advertising and they will also be willing to pay more if our magazine had less advertising." Key insights usually dismiss previous assumptions.

• Build the business impact: While key insights show you where to focus and help you identify some goals, the next step is to define a strategy to transform them into a positive business impact. In this phase, creativity is very important.

Even if it may seem that sensemaking is the key to solve all problems, its application is to be considered only in some specific cases. When you need to solve problems fast and/or on a large scale, you must rely on automated quantitative methods. If you have sound knowledge and experience on the issue, you should apply basic data analytics (sales of plane tickets are going down due to a competitor's promotion and you know that offering a similar discount will regain a part of the sales). If you are moderately familiar with the elements of the problem and can foresee several probable outcomes, then you can formulate sound hypotheses and test them with the adequate model (sales are going down in spite of our discounts, but we know that several possible explanations can be tested). Finally, when we are unfamiliar with the problem and we can't clearly identify possible outcomes or hypotheses, then we should rely on a different approach, such as sensemaking (we are losing money and we have no idea what is the possible reason). Be careful, since a common mistake is to think that you have possible explanations when in reality you have little knowledge about the problem and you should challenge your assumptions and hypotheses.

> **Box 11: Human Science Theories**
> The analytical approach of sensemaking is focused on human experience, abductive reasoning, and the use of human science theories. Examples of these theories are:
>
> - Think description: Description of elements that also includes their context in order to better define them and to be understandable to external people.
> - Double loop: A problem should be approached twice (or more times) leaving space for changing both the model and the established goals.
> - Semiotics: The use of signs and symbols to understand human behavior, taking into consideration that the same symbol can have different meanings for different people. A common business approach is to verify whether the meaning a company tries to communicate through a symbol corresponds to the meaning this symbol has for customers.
> - Mental models: This is based on the discourse theory according to which words acquire specific meanings depending on the context in which they are used. Mental models are patterns that explain how people experience the use of a product in a specific context. For example, drinking tea in the United States is associated with the meaning of "adding" since it can give extra energy, while in China it is associated with "subtraction" since it implies relaxation.

- Social systems: People tend to simplify reality using binary code (good vs. bad, cheap vs. expensive, gain vs. loss, success vs. failure) despite the many nuances a concept may have. This tendency creates important misunderstandings when we interact with people that use a different binary code for the same concept. This can happen, for example, when company managers are defining possible benefits for workers as expensive versus economic, while the workers are seeing them as useful versus useless.
- Nonverbal language: Nonverbal language can be more revealing then verbal language about people's underlying causes for choices and behavior.
- Psychology and Influence theories: You can use the theories explained in the chapter "Understand the Human Mind" to better understand the way people think and act.

Christian Madsbjerg and Mikkel B. Rasmussen presented an example of a European brewing company that was suffering from falling bar and pub sales. Conventional market research wasn't finding any explanation.[68] They started by reframing the problem focusing on the experience of bar clients, bartenders, and servers. A team of social anthropologists gathered several photographs, videos, and field notes. They dismissed the assumption that the promotional material (T-shirts, stickers, etc.) was valued by owners. Moreover, not only was the promotional material underused but it was also mocked. The personnel didn't know much about beer, and female servers resented having to be flirtatious and felt trapped in an unpleasant job. The response was to customize items for different bars and bar owners, to provide training and to offer taxi service for employees who worked late (especially female employees). Thanks to these measures, bar and pub sales rebounded.

---

68   Madsbjerg and Rasmussen, "An anthropologist..."

Quantitative Data Analysis

Since this book focuses on the qualitative side of data analysis, it is beyond its scope to describe inductive and deductive quantitative methods. However, I've decided to describe how we can improve quantitative data analysis by adding qualitative elements and by including prior probabilities (deductive approach) to traditional frequentist statistical analysis (inductive approach).

Despite the benefits of the increasing amounts of available data, the more we have of it, the more difficult it is to distinguish *noise from signal*. With so much data, several patterns will start to arise making it difficult to separate patterns created by chance, patterns you don't need, and the "signal" you need. Nate Silver explains in his book *The Signal and the Noise*[69] why many predictions fail and offer interesting suggestions to improve forecasts.

Predictions mainly fail for three reasons: uncertainty, complexity, and subjectivity. *Uncertainty* is intrinsic in predictions even if we tend to make certain statements about the future. Uncertainty affects different aspects of predictions. First, there is an initial uncertainty where the data you collect may be imprecise or biased. Second, there is a structural uncertainty due to the limits of our understanding of the phenomenon and the rules that govern it. Finally, there is a scenario uncertainty because we don't know whether the present trends will continue in the future or whether some event is going to occur. Take the example of the predictions about climate change. Even if it has been proved that the level of CO_2 affects the global temperature, forecasts about the actual increase in temperature during the next decades may be quite flawed due to the underlying uncertainties: (1) recorded temperatures are affected by many other phenomena besides CO_2 levels such as climate cycles, solar activity, or volcanoes (initial uncertainty); (2) in spite of having defined the relationship between CO_2 and temperature, the whole phenomenon is more

---

69   Nate Silver, *The Signal and the Noise: Why so Many Predictions Fail, but Some Don't* (New York: Penguin, 2012).

complex and its representation with models may be limited (structural uncertainty); (3) temperature estimations are made on the bases of CO_2 level estimations, but human activities could change, and therefore the increasing trend of CO_2 level could change (scenario uncertainty).

Even if you manage to effectively reduce initial and structural uncertainties, scenario uncertainty will always be present. Scenario uncertainty is worsened when what you have to predict is "out of the sample," that is, we don't have data about similar situations and we have to extrapolate the conclusions. Using a statistical example, imagine you estimate price elasticity with available data, which has a price range from 10€ to 30€ for a product, but your boss asks you to use the outcome to predict demand with a price of 50€. Maybe there is a turning point where demand drops to zero, or price elasticity changes radically after a certain price level.

Another problem for predictions is complexity. The *complexity* of the events we try to predict implies a double problem. On the one hand, it obliges us to approximate for the sake of practicality, but then we forget about this simplification and we think that the approximation is reality. On the other hand, when we increase models' complexity to reflect reality, we risk over-fitting them using noise (wrong patterns) instead of signals (useful patterns for our prediction).

Finally, all predictions have a certain level of subjectivity. *Subjectivity* makes predictions biased by our vision, ideas, principles, and past experiences. For example, when you only identify the patterns you are looking for or when you dismiss scenarios just because they are unfamiliar, but unfamiliarity doesn't mean that they are improbable.

The first step in improving predictions is to recognize our subjectivity, reduce our biases, and admit that there are things we don't know. However, it does not mean that you have to eliminate human judgment. You have to recognize your biases and use them to your advantage. *Human judgment* is very important since it can improve numerical models thanks to eyesight, experience, and knowledge. In his book, Nate Silver describes how meteorologists improved precipitations forecast by 25% and temperature forecasts by 10% thanks to human judgment. The human touch is also important for the *context* of a prediction, to see the big picture instead of getting lost in many details. Complexity can be dealt with by putting the phenomenon into a context and understanding *the theory behind it*. Weather forecasts are also quite successful because the "rules" by which weather works are reliably known and understood by meteorologists. The same is not true for economic forecasts whose rules are not very clear.

Data quality is another important point in improving predictions. Inaccuracy in collecting data can be reduced by improving sampling, improving measurement tools, or using data cleansing techniques. However, there is a limit to the accuracy you can reach. In weather forecasts, different scenarios are calculated by introducing modified input data to account for possible measurement inaccuracies. You also have to consider that when human behavior is involved results can be biased by self-reinforcement or self-cancellation. For example, when the media increases the frequency of news about a potentially dangerous flu, more cases are detected since more people ask to be diagnosed and doctors are more attentive to diagnose it.

Probably, one of the most important suggestions to improve forecasts is to use a probabilistic approach. Due to complexity and uncertainty, instead of forecasting a precise result, you should forecast the probability of an event or the probabilities of different scenarios. In practical terms, Nate Silver suggests using Bayes' theorem, which is based on prior and conditional probabilities. This method presents two main advantages. The first is that since you have to establish a prior probability, it obliges you to take into account the big picture. Second, it requires you to assign probabilities to events, which is a way to measure uncertainty. The author presents an example where a woman living with a partner finds a pair of underwear in her drawer which is not hers. The woman may jump to the conclusion that her partner is cheating on her. But if you use Bayes' theorem, the answer will be quite different. First, you define the prior probability—that is how likely it is that the partner is cheating on her. Then you have the new event: she has found a pair of underwear. Here, you define the probability of her finding the underwear in case the partner is really cheating on her and the probability in case he is not cheating on her. Once you calculate the posterior probability, you will find that the probability of the partner cheating on her is only 29%. Notice that prior probability is critical in defining posterior probability. In fact, when prior probability is low, we tend to make false-positive judgments (he is cheating) since we give too much weight to the new event (underwear appearing). This tendency can be exploited to your advantage, for example, in gambling, when people or bookmakers put too much weight on recent events and forget about prior probabilities.

PRIOR PROBABILITY		
How likely it is that he is cheating on you	x	4%
NEW EVENT: UNDERWEAR ARE FOUND		
Probability of underwear appearing if he is cheating on you	y	50%
Probability of underwear appearing if he is NOT cheating on you	z	5%
POSTERIOR PROBABILITY		
How likely it is that he is cheating on you, given that you have found the underwear	$\dfrac{xy}{xy + z(1-x)}$	29%

Figure 29: Example of Bayes' theorem (Source: Adapted from Nate Silver, The Signal and the Noise)

Figure 29 presents an example of how to solve the problem. Alternatively, you can also use a double entry table, where on one hand you have "cheating/not cheating" and on the other hand you have "underwear found/underwear not found."[70] Remember that the probability you are assigning to events or outcomes must not represent your confidence about the forecast, but it has to represent the probability of them occurring.

---

70   For more information, check chapter 42 "Bayesian Approach to Hypothesis Testing" of my book *80 Fundamental Models for Business Analysts* (see Bibliography).

The method of conditional probabilities can be used for more complex problems where you have to establish several prior probabilities to slice down a complex problem into smaller, simpler ones. Philip Tetlock in his book[71] *Superforecasting* proposes the use of the "Fermi estimation" to tackle complex prediction problems. This method consists of dividing a big problem into small estimations starting from the most general: the outside view. In my book *80 Fundamental Models for Business Analysts*, I briefly explained this technique:

It consists of breaking down a problem into several probability questions to make more accurate guesses and then adding up those questions that will produce a more realistic final outcome. This technique usually starts by taking into consideration an outer perspective. For example, we are presented with a picture of a family and we have to predict whether they have a pet or not. Instinctively we may start by focusing on the family's characteristics that we can identify. However, we should start with a broader perspective, for example the number of families in a certain geographical space (country, state, city, etc.) who own pets, namely 30%. This is our starting point, so we know without any other additional information that our best guess would be that there is a 30% probability that this family owns a pet. We can then adjust our prediction with an inside view focusing on the family's characteristics, for example age, ethnicity, children, and so on. A famous example is the estimation of the number of piano tuners in Chicago. Instead of guessing the number directly, the problem is broken down into several questions, starting with defining the total population of the city, then determining the number of households, guessing the number of households with a piano, gauging how often a piano needs to be tuned, and so on.[72]

---

71   Philip E. Tetlock and Dan Gardner, *Superforecasting: The Art and Science of Prediction* (New York: Crown, 2016).
72   Alberto Scappini, *Fundamental Models for Business Analysts*.

According to the author of *Superforecasting*, another element that improves forecasts is to weight the opinion of several people. This is because different people have different information, use different models, and have different biases that can level each other out when put together. You should, therefore, look for *consensus*, especially if you are not very confident about your forecast. However, remember that even if you look for consensus or an average of forecasts of different people, it doesn't necessarily mean that results will be good. Moreover, to make biases cancel themselves, forecasts must be independent; otherwise, you will have the opposite effect, that is, you will reinforce your biases. Finally, remember that using averaged forecasts does not imply that it will be better than each individual forecast; it means that it will be usually better than the average individual forecast.

ANALYTICS

Analytics is probably the best option in two situations. The first situation is when there's an unclear question to the problem, which means that you have not defined the frame of decision-making. In this situation, the process of analytics (a.k.a. data mining or exploratory data analysis) may lead you to define the question and the frame of decision-making. Then you can perform inductive or deductive data analysis. The second situation is when, despite the availability of data, its characteristics and/or the level of uncertainty doesn't allow applying inductive, deductive, or machine learning analyses.

An important difference with other statistical analyses is that you can't directly infer something based on the available data (like inferential statistics), but the conclusions you make must be only about what you can observe in the available data. Of course, then you will need to use this knowledge to make decisions, and therefore you are in a certain way inferring something, but if you receive for example a bad review about your product you can't infer that customers' satisfaction is lowering. This piece of information should be analyzed just for what it is and decisions should be made based on that. The difference may be subtle, but it is important to remember that you mustn't make conclusions in the same way as you were when applying inferential statistics with a representative sample.

The process of analytics can be merely descriptive, but you will usually be looking for patterns and/or anomalies using mainly charts, pivot tables, and descriptive statistics tools. Patterns are based on repetition, which can be observed either on time evolution (e.g., seasonality) or correlations (e.g., a certain product is mainly bought by certain customers). Anomalies are exceptions to the average situation and can identify an interesting event (e.g., sales skyrocketed on the first of June due to a viral user comment on Instagram). To find patterns and anomalies, you compare different descriptive statistics (sum, count, average, range, variance, minimum, maximum, frequency distribution, etc.) among different categories or you analyze the evolution of these statistics over time. The comparison can be done using absolute numbers, or by modifying them, for example by calculating the absolute difference, the percentage difference, the share of the total, and so forth. Besides, categories can be filtered, grouped, and sorted. Finally, business knowledge is fundamental in analytics since it helps you correctly interpret what you observe. For example, knowing that there is a distribution problem makes you discard the hypothesis of decreasing demand for your product.

HEURISTICS

While in "Understand the Human Mind," I was focusing on the systematic errors of heuristics, now I will focus on their usefulness. I will mainly use the work of Gerd Gigerenzer despite his strong critic of Amos Tversky and Daniel Kahneman. I'm absolutely not qualified to judge the work of these great minds, but in my opinion, the critics don't diminish the astonishing work of the two Jewish psychologists. Their work and the work of those who followed shed light on the limitation of the human mind in judgment and choices. This is fundamental if you want to use heuristics. But also, I wanted to focus on the advantages of heuristics, and the work of Gigerenzer, among others, is quite interesting.[73]

In highly complex and uncertain situations, the use of simple heuristics can outperform the use of complex models. Heuristics are sort of rules of thumb used either consciously (simple rules) or unconsciously (intuition). They are based on experience and their effectiveness depends on their adaptation to the environment, namely a business problem or a choice situation. An example of heuristics is to identify an inactive customer based on the time of the last purchase instead of relying on a complex optimization model. While the goal of prediction models is to optimize the situation, the goal of heuristics is to satisfice, namely achieving a good solution instead of the best solution. In addition, the flexibility and subjectivity of heuristics foster creativity and innovation.

The advantage of heuristics is that they ignore part of the complexity, and this means not only less effort, but also a lower estimation error in uncertain environments. An example is the experiment performed with German and U.S. students[74] who were asked to identify the larger city between Detroit and Milwaukee. Here, 90% of German students versus 60% of U.S. students answered correctly using the "recognition heuristic," that is, they chose Detroit for the simple fact of having heard about this city.

Usually, when we compare different prediction models, we talk about the effort-accuracy tradeoff. This is only partly true when you use heuristics under uncertainty. Under risk (where the probability of outcomes can be estimated), the use of heuristics can be an alternative to more complex models since it implies less resources and time, at the expense of accuracy. However, under absolute uncertainty, this principle doesn't hold, and it is replaced by the principles of less-is-more: limiting infor-

---

73   For more information about heuristics, read *Heuristic Decision Making* by Gigerenzer and Gaissmaier; *Homo Heuristicus and the Bias-Variance Dilemma* by Brighton and Gigerenzer; and *Thinking, Fast and Slow* by Daniel Kahneman (see Bibliography).

74   Daniel G. Goldstein and Gerd Gigerenzer, "Models of Ecological Rationality: The Recognition Heuristic," *Psychological Review* 109, no. 1 (2002): 75–90.

mation and search leads to higher accuracy.[75] To explain this principle, I need to introduce the different components of error in predictions. Error is composed of bias, variance, and noise. Bias is the deviation from the reality (or, in mathematical terms, the difference between the predicting function and the function representing the reality); variance is caused by the peculiarities of specific samples, it increases as the sample size decreases; noise is the observing error in sampling. Simpler models tend to have a higher bias, since they are less accurate in detecting smaller variations. However, if you try to reduce bias by using more complex models, variance will increase since your model will tend to overfit the data. Overfitted models are less accurate in the prediction of future events. Besides, more information sometimes means more noise in the data. Heuristics implies a certain degree of bias that has some beneficial effect on controlling variance. We can say that it is the very fact of ignoring part of the information that produces a better result thanks to the reduction of variance. Therefore, since heuristics does not convey any advantage on bias compared to other models, their power relies on reducing variance.

At this point, after having praised the advantages of heuristics, I have to stop and be clear on one thing. Heuristics are not better than fact-based decisions or statistical models when data is available, and the level of uncertainty is manageable. What I'm saying is that you can't just "guess" how many customers are happy with your product, when, with a small sample and an inexpensive survey, you can obtain quite an accurate answer. Moreover, heuristics don't perform better when strong biases are in place. These can be personal biases (based on people's experience) or information biases, for example, those produced by the news. The frequency of a certain type of news makes us think the phenomenon is larger than realty. For example, if during a certain period, several pieces of news are published about immigrants committing crimes, people will tend to overstate the number of immigrants present

---

75   Henry Brighton and Gerd Gigerenzer, "Homo Heuristicus and the Bias–Variance Dilemma," *Action, Perception and the Brain* (2012): 68–91.

in the country or the share of crimes committed by them compared to nationals. In conclusion, you should use heuristics when no data model is suitable for the situation. Besides, even if heuristics is the best option or you use it to complement data models, you must be aware of the possible biases (see "Understand the Human Mind" chapter). Intuition is powerful but subject to overconfidence and biases. To avoid this, heuristics must be applied using structured methods, for example, by adding prior probabilities to the estimation or by evaluating attributes separately in a job interview instead of making a global evaluation (I will explain these two techniques in detail).

Here, I introduce some of the techniques you can use to exploit the advantages of heuristics by limiting their main side effects.

INTUITION

Intuition is based on the recognition of past events and the application of what we have learned from them to the new situation. When intuition is based on true experience and skills, it is very useful, for example for firefighters or chess players. However, if intuition is the result of substitution (of a complex question with a simpler one) and overconfidence, the result is inaccurate. But then, when do we use intuition? Daniel Kahneman and Gary Klein wrote a paper on this.[76] According to them, we can trust intuition when the environment is sufficiently regular to be predictable, and when these regularities can be learned during a prolonged period of time. The second point implies that after making a decision, the feedback has to be available and with a short delay. Examples where intuition works are in sport where you have immediate feedback and you learn what works and what doesn't. In economics, however, intuition tends not to work because the environment is quite unpredictable and feedback is ambiguous and delayed. When dealing with business issues, usually pure intuition won't work, so you have to apply some rules and numbers if you want to use heuristics. Daniel Kahneman proposed a method to avoid

---

76   Daniel Kahneman and Gary Klein, "Conditions for Intuitive Expertise: A Failure to Disagree," *American Psychologist* 64, no. 6 (2009): 515–26.

extreme predictions based on weak evidence. Imagine that you have to predict the outcome of a promotional campaign:

1. Identify the criteria for defining a campaign similar to this one and select similar campaigns.
2. Calculate the average outcome of these campaigns. This represents the prior probability (also called statistical base rate or outside view), which is the starting point of your estimation. Say an average ROI of 10%. If you had no more information, 10% would be your best estimate.
3. Estimate the outcome based on the evidence you have, namely the specific information about the campaign. You are investing a lot more than other campaigns and you estimate a 50% ROI.
4. Estimate the correlation between the evidence you have and the outcome, that is, the impact investment has on success, let's say 25%.
5. Move from the prior probability toward your estimation proportionally to the size of the correlation. In our example, you move 25% * (50% − 10%) = 10%; your final estimate is 20% ROI.

Another interesting method Kahneman suggested is related to interviews. Instead of asking a general judgment to the interviewers about a candidate, ask them to evaluate different attributes separately, preferably with a predefined scale (e.g., from 1 to 5). Then, use simple statistics; for example the number of attributes above 4, or the average score, based on the results of previous interviews. Intuition is important at assessing individual attributes, but by avoiding an overall judgment we avoid possible biases such as the halo effect, confirmation bias, or representativeness.

RECOGNITION HEURISTIC
The underlying assumption is that the recognized alternative has the highest value. It has been proven to be particularly useful when you want to test small categories in samples. In this situation, you would need a huge sample to obtain significant conclusions in statistics. This heuristic has

been tested to predict political elections where results were estimated using party names recognition compared to asking voting intention to voters.[77] Recognition heuristics was competitive with voting intention in predicting results for smaller parties. Voting intention using statistical sampling techniques is competitive if the sample is representative and the share of votes is not too small (1% in a sample of 1000 people). However, when sample size is smaller, the sample is not representative, or the share of votes is too low, using recognition-based heuristics should be preferred. In this example, the problem was to predict the difference in vote intention between large parties, since they were all quite well recognized. A solution is to use the wisdom of the crowd by asking them to predict elections results. Estimations were accurate and using this method not only implies using voters' recognition of parties, but also includes other information (for example, a radical party may be quite famous for their extreme ideas, but people know that the voting intention will be limited).

FLUENCY HEURISTIC
When both (or several) alternatives are recognized or when you don't have a defined set of alternatives, you may infer that the one that is recognized faster has the highest value. This heuristic works when the difference in the time necessary for recalling is clearly different between the alternatives. In the case of not having a defined set of alternatives, the first alternative recalled is the best one.

ONE-CLEVER-CUE
With this heuristic, you just use a critical cue to make a decision. We are instinctually using this kind of heuristic when we have to catch a ball. In this case, our clever-cue is maintaining a constant optical angle between us and the ball. One-clever-cue heuristic is helpful when weight and redundancy of cues are quite variable and sample size is small. It has

77   W. Gaissmaier and Julian N. Marewski, "Forecasting Elections with Mere Recognition from Lousy Samples: A Comparison of Collective Recognition, Wisdom of Crowds, and Representative Polls," *Judgement and Decision Making* (2011).

been proven to be effective in detecting criminal location by drawing a circle that includes all the sites of crime. This method is more accurate than complex algorithms when the number of crimes is small.

TAKE-THE-BEST

This heuristic is based on three steps. First, you unconditionally[78] order possible cues according to their validity (how well a cue can correctly predict). Second, you start from the best cue and stop at the first cue that is able to discriminate between the choices. Third, you choose the alternative suggested by the discriminant cue. Take-the-best performs better when cue validities are skewed and the interrelations between the cues are uncertain. The very simplicity of this method makes it perform better than multiple regressions under the abovementioned circumstances. In consumer choices, for example, take-the-best can make good predictions especially in the early stages of the decision process when we have many alternatives and cues (i.e., product characteristics and customers' preferences).

FAST-AND-FRUGAL TREE

When the number of cues increases, a Bayes approach to a tree model requires much more calculation; it increases estimation error due to the limited number of data points for each leaf of the tree (e.g., using binary cues, the tree has 2^c leaves, where c is the number of binary cues). Instead, with a fast-and-frugal tree with binary cues, we have $c + 1$ leaves, improving its robustness and simplicity. Cues are ranked in a predetermined order, and you stop adding cues when they lead to an exit or when any additional cue would help to better discriminate between the alternatives. This method has shown to be competitive with logistic regression in medicine, sports, and economics. Figure 30 shows a hypothetical

78 Cues are ordered not taking into consideration their interdependencies, a factor that may vary their validity but that requires more complex calculations and increases possible errors.

example of a fast-and-frugal tree to classify customers by their value to the company. The goal is to focus the limited commercial resources only on the most valuable active customers.

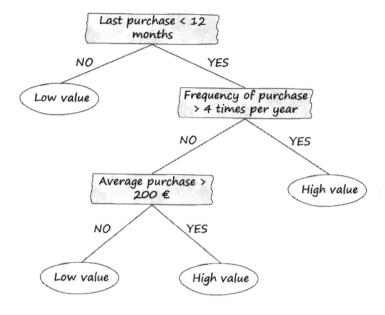

Figure 30: Example of a fast-and-frugal tree

TALLYING

Compared to take-the-best heuristic, which considers only one cue, tallying takes into consideration all cues (or a certain number of cues out of the total). Cues have equal weight and the selected alternative is the one with the most favorable cues. If you get a draw, add one more cue, and if no cue is found you just guess. Tallying performs better than multiple regression when the ratio of alternatives to cues is small (10 or lower), R^2 is low ($R^2 \leq 0.5$), and cues are highly redundant.[79] Using the previous example, we can define a high-value customer if it has at least two out of

---

79   G. Gigerenzer and Wolfgang Gaissmaier, "Heuristic Decision Making," *Annual Review of Psychology* (2011).

the three cues (the last purchase within the past twelve months, an average purchase of 200€, and at least four purchases per year on average).

1/N RULE
This is a very simple heuristics to solve problems of resource allocation in case of high uncertainty, little information, small samples, and large population. According to the 1/N rule, each alternative receives the same share of value. It has been proven to be fairly competitive compared to more complex models in allocating financial resources.

SOCIAL HEURISTICS
Social heuristics are based on other actors of the environment. For example, "wisdom of the crowd" exploits the collective knowledge of a group of people whose averaged responses are proven to give quite good predictions, as explained also by Gardner and Tetlock in *Superforecasting*[80] Other examples concern imitating the majority, choosing the default option, or imitating the most successful (e.g., the best competitor).

---

80   Tetlock and Gardner, *Superforecasting*.

Unpredictable Events (Black Swans)

In Europe, before 1697, it was believed that all swans were white because every swan ever spotted or examined was white. However, this belief unexpectedly changed after a Dutch explorer found black swans in Australia. Nassim Nicholas Taleb[81] used this metaphor for highly improbable and unpredictable events that have an important impact. Like black swans, because you haven't seen these events, it doesn't mean they don't exist.

The author argues against the optimism in forecasting presented for example in *Superforecasting*, explaining why predictions concerning complex outcomes are doomed to fail due to the unpredictability of Black Swans. Human simplification mechanisms that allow as to survive have some costs when we try to predict future events. First, we tend to ignore the complexity of things by creating a coherent story to explain what happened. This creates confirmation biases and a general underestimation of randomness. For example, we tend to attribute the success of a businessman to the efforts taken, determination, and so forth, but we completely underestimate the effect of luck. For this one success story, there may be many more about people that failed. Another problem is that we are not comfortable thinking in terms of probabilities and we tend to judge performance based on results instead of judging it based on the cost of the alternative.

However, even if we can think probabilistically, the author says[82], Black Swans make these probabilities quite unprecise. When we pass from theory to reality, we have two main problems:

- Inverse problem: In real life, we don't observe distributions but a series of events, some of which are so rare that either we need

81   Among other books, author of *Fooled by Randomness* and *The Black Swan* (see Bibliography).

82   Nassim Nicholas Taleb, *The Black Swan: The Impact of the Highly Improbable* (New York: Random House Trade Paperbacks, 2010).

so much time to properly estimate the probability of their occurrence or we haven't yet seen them.

- Pre-asymptotics: This problem arises when we try to apply some theory derived from idealized situations to real situations. When outcomes are complex and the probability distribution of events is unpredictable and extreme, this problem compromises forecasts.

To identify these highly uncertain situations, we first have to distinguish between risk and uncertainty. Both imply a certain degree of uncertainty, but under risk we can use available information to define a model able to optimize the outcome. This is possible because we can logically deduce the mechanism behind the outcome and its probability can be estimated. On the other hand, under a higher degree of uncertainty, the set of options and outcomes is open and they are highly subjective. This means that there isn't an objectively optimal solution, even if we analyze the situation a posteriori. Borrowing the concept made popular by Donald Rumsfeld, we can say that we are in the presence of unknown unknowns because under uncertainty there are things that we don't know we don't know.

In the article "The Fourth Quadrant: A Map of the Limits of Statistics,"[83] Taleb shows a double-entry matrix about the robustness of statistics in different situations. On the one hand, we have the type of decision that can be simple (usually binary, for example "true" vs. "false" and where the important thing is the probability associated) or complex (the probability is not only important, so is the impact, and this adds an additional layer of uncertainty). Examples of simple decisions/payoffs are medicine, games, bets, and bankruptcy. Examples of complex decisions/payoffs are terrorism, catastrophes, climate, finance, and economy. The other variable of the matrix concerns the type of distribution or the probability structure. On one hand, we have the "Mediocristan," which can be

---

83   https://www.edge.org/conversation/nassim_nicholas_taleb-the-fourth-quadrant-a-map-of-the-limits-of-statistics

represented by normal distribution (namely the Gaussian distribution—the "bell curve") and where the occurrence of an exception has little impact on the distribution itself. An example is if you take the average height of a group of people and a very tall person is added to the sample. In this case, the distribution won't change radically. On the other hand, we have the "Extremistan" where the occurrence of exceptions has an upsetting impact on the distribution. For instance, suppose you are calculating distribution of the average income of a group of people and you add a millionaire to the group. When decisions are simple and distributions are "Mediocristan," statistics works quite well (first quadrant), while in the fourth quadrant statistics is quite fragile to Black Swans.

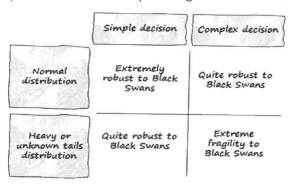

Figure 31: Matrix of the robustness/limits of statistics to Black Swans (Source: Adapted from Nicholas Taleb[81])

To be prepared for unpredictable events, you can think about the less obvious events, preparing yourself to benefit from positive Black Swans and, at the same time, hedge against negative ones. To prepare for highly improbable events, you can use a "scenario" approach. Instead of relying on the most probable scenario, perform what-if analysis using extreme hypothesis to define one or several best and worst scenarios. For example, in a worst scenario of sales prediction for the next year, you can imagine an economic crisis, that your provider will double the price, that clients will lose interest in your product, and so forth. A way to prove your assumptions and hypothesis at an extreme is to use the method of Red Teams (see box 12).

Box 12: Red Teams

We are often too self-confident and biased by our beliefs, entourage, company's culture, and so forth, that we are not able to detect possible weaknesses in our strategies or analyses. To overcome this problem (and to consider rare but impactful events, namely Black Swans), we can use a technique called "Red Teams"[84] (in military jargon) where someone is playing the devil's advocate trying to find possible vulnerabilities. These teams must be external or at least take an external point of view in order to avoid internal biases that prevent them from discovering weaknesses. In addition, they should be composed of the right mix of people, most importantly people able to think unconventionally, to challenge the authority, and to change their way of acting. Red teams have to change their strategies, because if they become predictable, the opposite team will adapt to it.

More practically, to implement this method you can use simulations where an external or internal team assumes the role of competitors or customers and challenges the strategy proposed. An alternative technique, which can be also used to challenge your predictions or analyses, is called "alternative analysis." It implies testing the results in a range of scenarios, for example using what-if analysis, brainstorming, and so forth.

---

84   Micah Zenko, *Red Team: How to Succeed by Thinking Like the Enemy* (New York: Basic Books, 2015).

Machine Learning

The huge amount of data combined with the increasing processing power of computers is improving the possibilities of data analytics. As I said before, machine learning is about giving an answer based on many examples instead of relying on instructions, and this is only possible when you dispose of a certain number of examples. Besides some obvious benefits, there are also some risks and the data artist must be able to both understand the possibilities of it and, at the same time, not to rely completely on raw data and pure quantitative data analysis.

There are three main advantages in exploiting the so-called big data:[85]

- Statistical analysis relies on random sampling to increase accuracy; however, this is the second-best option. With big data, you can use almost the whole data set, this being the best option to increase accuracy. Moreover, with sampling, you will be able to drill down data into subcategories only to a certain level; whereas, disposing of the whole data set means you are free to perform deeper analyses.
- Instead of trying to dispose of a few precise data points (in which case a bad measurement can have important implications), with big data you use a lot of less precise data points. Even if individual data points are not very precise, the big picture will be more accurate than the one given by a few data points.
- Using big data is about the "what" instead of the "why" of things; therefore instead of trying to prove the causality (usually quite difficult to prove), it could be more effective just to prove the correlation (the "what"). Due to the amount of data and the frequency of updates, just knowing what happens (correlation) could be enough (at least in some cases).

---

85   Viktor Mayer-Schönberger and Kenneth Cukier, *Big Data: A Revolution That Will Transform How We Live, Work, and Think* (London: John Murray, 2013).

Chris Anderson suggested in 2008 the theory of *The End of Theory*[86] according to which with massive data no theory or model will be necessary anymore, but the numbers will speak for themselves. Liberating science from the rigid deductive method of "theory – test – model," more discoveries will be made since the actual models are constrained and flawed.

It is beyond the purpose of this book to explain in detail how to exploit machine learning, but data analysts must be knowledgeable about when it is advisable to use it and the advantages it can give.

---

86   Chris Anderson, "The End of Theory: The Data Deluge Makes the Scientific Method Obsolete," *Wired* (2008).

Be a Negotiator

Data analysts probably won't deal with complex negotiations, but they may have to negotiate a service with a consultant or external provider or negotiate goals, deadlines, and other elements of an analytics project, or simply negotiate supply of data from other departments. In any case, having some basic knowledge of negotiation may end up saving you time and improving the result.

The aim of any negotiation is to obtain the maximum value from it, but without compromising long-term value. For example, cheating in order to get a better deal may give you higher short-term value, but it will undermine the relationship and future deals.

Negotiations can be very complex, but I like to visualize them in three simple steps:

- Define your goals and your value reserve.
- Define the real interests and the value reserve of the counterpart.
- Obtain the maximum possible value.

First, you have to clearly define what you need in detail: (1) *Clearly write down your goals.* Don't be too generic—for example "I need data on competitors' prices"—but clearly define the perimeter (which competitors, for which items, how often, etc.) and other important characteristics such as how reliable the data should be or if you value the volume of data more than its quality. Always start with the end in mind; for example, think about how you will be using this new data in your analysis. When you define the value you want from the negotiation, define it in the broader possible way taking into consideration the overall value of the deal, and not only the value of some direct benefits you can obtain. In addition, think carefully to your best alternative or BATNA,[87] in order to know the point at which you are better off by leaving the negotiation, namely when no deal is the best deal. It is far better to use the concept of BATNA instead of using, for example, a "bottom line," below which you

---

[87] "Best Alternative to a Negotiated Agreement," described by Roger Fisher, William Ury, and Bruce Patton in *Getting to Yes* (see Bibliography).

automatically opt for the "no deal" option. Bottom lines may be too low, and therefore will make you accept worse deals, or they may be too high and force you to refuse a deal even if it was your best option.

The second step is to: (2) *gather as more information as possible about the other part.* This will help you define their real interests, and not just the superficial demands they may have. Also try to understand who they are, how they like to meet or to conduct a negotiation, find out the "why" of their demands and responses, and not just the "what." This means instead of negotiating on positions, you should negotiate on interests. For example, imagine you are asking for sales data from your sales department. You need detailed data but people do not seem to be very cooperative and are slowly providing you incomplete data. So you talk to different people and discover that the reason for this situation is that they consider your study to be doubting their work. In this case, you should talk to them, clearly explaining the goal of your study, showing some rough work, and assuring that you won't make it public before their approval.

You have to keep in mind that their problems are also your problems because they will impact your deal. Hence, it is very important not only to understand their constraints but also to help your counterpart to overcome them. You have to find the common ground where your interests meet, but if the other part has difficulties to define theirs, you should help them instead of taking advantage of it (short-term advantage!).

Don't limit your search for information to your counterpart but amplify it. If you are negotiating with an external provider, find out how much other providers charge, what other clients say about them, and so forth. Also, try to not focus narrowly on the available information since this can create "blind spots," namely some hidden relevant information that can completely change the value balance of your deal. For example, imagine you are negotiating a service for competitors' web scraping, but a new law that bans this practice is about to be approved.

Finally, you have to (3) *obtain the maximum value from the negotiation.* According to old school definition, a negotiation is a zero-sum game; therefore, in order to "win," you must squeeze your enemy to get most of the value on the table and leave the least of it. However, this approach limits a lot the value you can get in a negotiation. Instead, think about the negotiation as a win-win game, where the value on the table can be increased for both parties. To do this, a good technique is to negotiate simultaneously about different items and find those with unequal value for the parties. For example, a few years ago with a new job position, I inherited an old contract about the supply of competitors' pricing data. It was not expensive for the data we received, but there were some issues concerning the quality. Therefore, we asked for proposals to other suppliers and one, in particular, promised the data reliability and quality we were looking for. However, the problem was the price. We couldn't afford the new price, and the supplier could not provide what we asked at the price we could afford. In the beginning, I thought that we had to stick to our old contract, but then I had an informal chat with them and I discovered that the problem was the tracking of a specific part of the prices. For them it was critical to reduce these kinds of prices, while for us, these specific kinds of prices were not so critical, so we could drastically reduce it. Finally, by just reducing a small part of the amount of data provided, we had a better deal with high-quality data at a lower price than the previous contract.

If you find something your counterpart values a lot, but for you, it is not so important, trading on it will increase the overall value of the deal. The opposite is also valid, namely trading something very valuable for you, but not so critical for the other party.

Once you have exploited all possibilities of increasing the overall value, you have to obtain the maximum value from the deal, without compromising your relationship with the other part or compromising future agreements. The first thing to do is clearly separate the person from the problem. You must make it clear that you are going to be tough on the problem, but soft on your counterpart. This also means that if you feel attacked, you don't have to respond by attacking or defending yourself, but you should stick to your plan, listen to the other part, and focus on the problem, not on the person. Second, you need to make the counterpart understand and value the real value you are putting on the table.

Your credibility plays an important role, and this emerges mainly from past experiences, your relationship with the other party, and how you present yourself. You must look always confident about your goals and what you are saying. The way you present or frame your project, offer, or proposal is critical. Information must flow clearly and easily in both directions, and in case of possible misunderstanding, you have to take a pause and ask for clarifications before going on. Reinforce your idea by providing on one side logical evidence of the benefits for the other part (e.g., by establishing objective criteria on which to negotiate), but also connecting emotionally. For example, if you are proposing a certain analytical project to your boss, you can provide logical evidence of the problem it tackles, but at the same time, you can connect emotionally with him or her by addressing some sensitive issue. However, keep in mind that not only your counterpart's opinion might be biased, but yours too. Usually, we tend to be too overconfident about our proposal and we tend not to see where we are wrong. Be humble and objectively evaluate your proposal, better with the help of a "devil's advocate" who always tries to question it.

Overconfidence is not the only problem. There are also "cognitive biases," which distort your vision of reality. For example, if the conversation becomes too emotional, you may not make the best decisions, or if the counterpart sets a wrong reference point, then all the conversation will be biased in his or her favor. Imagine you need some data from the IT department. At the beginning of the conversation, they overstate the time needed to extract this kind of data and exaggerate on the amount of work they have. If everybody agrees on that, then all the negotiations will be biased. Be prepared in these situations by being well informed and able to neutralize these biases. Be also aware that people can be irrational and emotional, in which case logic may not be useful. In these cases, you have first to understand their emotions, be emphatic and respectful, and try to understand the reasons for their emotions. Only then, you can try to lower the emotional level by providing more information and try to reason with logic.

Finally, a good negotiator knows when not to negotiate, namely when undertaking a negation can have negative effects on relationships, when he or she knows the alternatives are awful, or the effort needed in the negotiation is higher than the benefits to be obtained.

Since the data analyst must be creative, his or her ideas may be in general less orthodox and they may be more difficult to be accepted. However, if you need some sort of funding or the approval of your superiors, you must find a way to pass through your idea otherwise all the creative effort will be worth nothing. You can use two main techniques to make other people gradually accept your innovative idea:[88]

- Exposure effect: Since people get used to things to which they are exposed again and again, start exposing it little by little but constantly.
- Common points: Emphasize those points of your idea that your audience is familiar with, maybe because they worked in other situations. In this way, your idea will be more familiar and more easily accepted.

If you want to further investigate this subject, I suggest you read the book *Getting to Yes* (see Bibliography).

88   Grant and Sandberg, *Originals*.

Be a Communicator

You may carry on the best analysis ever, and you may have the most revealing insights, but if you can't properly communicate them, all your effort will be useless. Properly communicating results means that your audience will both understand them and want to take action on them.

To properly communicate, it is important to follow some simple principles on how to manage conversations. Then, you have to be aware of the context in which the communication will take place, namely who is your audience, what you want them to do, how you will do that, and so forth. Moreover, a good analyst should be able to add some "art" to the basics of decent communication. Hence, I've included a part on storytelling. Finally, the analyst has to master the main tools of communication: writing, speaking, and design. Special emphasis will be placed on data visualization since this topic is particularly relevant to the data analyst.

Principles

There are many books and sources of information about communication, but I've found one particularly simple and useful since it explains a series of principles that we can apply to better manage all kinds of communications.[89] I will briefly explain those principles but to gain more insights I suggest you read *How to Win Friends and Influence People* (see Bibliography).

TECHNIQUES IN HANDLING PEOPLE

1. Don't criticize, condemn, or complain. If you do, the other party may get defensive or even fight back. Try instead to understand the other's point of view.
2. Give honest and sincere appreciation. When they deserve it, show your appreciation and they will be more eager to listen to you and to what you want them to do.
3. Arouse an eager want in the other person. Instead of presenting an idea as yours, make the other person reason and come up with the same idea. The difference is that the other person will be more eager to carry on that idea.

WAYS TO MAKE PEOPLE LIKE YOU

1. Become genuinely interested in other people. Spend time and energy in knowing them better, in remembering little details that they will appreciate.
2. Smile. Smiling generates an automatic positive reaction.
3. Remember that a person's name is to that person the most important sound in any language. So remember people's names, and use them in conversations.

---

89   Dale Carnegie, *How to Win Friends and Influence People* (New York: Pocket Books, 1998; first published in 1937).

4. Be a good listener. Encourage others to talk about themselves. People love to talk about themselves and if you are a good listener they will perceive you as a good communicator, even if you haven't said a word.
5. Talk in terms of the other person's interests. Identify what other people are passionate about, get informed if needed, and talk about that with them. You will win their attention and appreciation.
6. Make the other person feel important and do it sincerely. Talk to people about themselves, about their achievements and strengths.

HOW TO WIN PEOPLE TO YOUR WAY OF THINKING

1. The only way to get the best of an argument is to avoid it. Arguing with somebody usually makes them more convinced of their points of view instead of getting them closer to yours.
2. Show respect for the other person's opinions. Never say, "You're wrong." If you think somebody is wrong, don't say it directly, but try to be diplomatic, say something like "I may be wrong, but I thought that . . ."
3. If you are wrong, admit it quickly and emphatically. This will give you respect and it may even make the other person take your defense. Presenting excuses or trying to avoid your responsibility generates the opposite reaction.
4. Begin in a friendly way. If you begin in an unfriendly way, the conversation will start with the other person getting defensive or aggressive.
5. Get the other person saying "yes" immediately. Before getting a "yes" to your argument, start by easier "sub-arguments" toward which your audience can't really disagree with. After a series of "yeses," you can finally state your main argument improving the odds of obtaining a positive answer.

6. Let the other person do a great deal of the talking. As explained before, be a good listener and let the other talk more.
7. Let the other person feel that the idea is his or hers. As mentioned earlier, this creates an eager want in the other person.
8. Try honestly to see things from the other person's point of view. Even if the other person is wrong, there is a reason for that point of view. Try to understand it and be tolerant.
9. Be sympathetic with the other person's ideas and desires. Don't blame anybody for feeling or saying something but try to understand the reasons why.
10. Appeal to the nobler motives. For example, if somebody didn't give what promised, you can reply with "I think you are a sincere and extremely honest person, so I want to believe you really tried to do that but you can't because . . ." Appealing to nobler motives creates a need in the other person to respect these motives.
11. Dramatize your ideas. Dramatizing your ideas a little bit increases your audience's attention and interest.
12. Throw down a challenge. Challenges are proved to improve motivation in performing certain tasks.

HOW TO CHANGE PEOPLE WITHOUT GIVING OR AROUSING RESENTMENT

1. Begin with praise and honest appreciation. Before calling the attention, start with a "candy," with a sort of "anesthesia," to soften the rest of the conversation.
2. Draw attention to people's mistakes indirectly. After the praise, avoid using the word "but" to start drawing the attention. Instead, you may say something like "I really appreciate how you improved in being more organized, and I think that if you keep improving it . . ." This is usually better than saying: "I really appreciate how

you improved in being more organized, but you have to further improve it."

3. Talk about your own mistakes before criticizing the other person. Admit that you are not perfect or superior, and you'll get more legitimacy in criticizing other people's mistakes.

4. Ask questions instead of giving direct orders. Instead of saying "Do this study," say "What do you think about this study? Can you think about some alternative study?"

5. Let the other person save face. Even if somebody has made a terrible mistake, try to make him or her save face. You won't obtain anything if the other person loses face.

6. Praise the slightest improvement and praise every improvement. This increases the other person's self-esteem and motivation.

7. Give the other person a fine reputation to live up to. If you want someone to improve a certain characteristic, build a good reputation about it and they will work hard to improve it.

8. Use encouragement. Make the fault seem easy to correct. This will improve motivation.

9. Make the other person happy about doing the thing you suggest. This is not always easy, but try to present it in a pleasant way, involve them in the decision process, explain the importance of doing it, state what they can obtain from it, and create the best circumstances and ambiance.

Context

Before undertaking any kind of data communication, you have to consider the context. To do that, you have to answer three main questions: Who is my audience? What is the purpose of the visualization? How do I transmit the information?[90]

Define who your audience is, what their needs and expectations are, their knowledge and capabilities, and how they perceive you (if you already have their esteem and consideration, you won't need to establish them in your presentation). Whenever possible, don't choose an audience with many interests and different needs, since you risk satisfying nobody. In case this is not possible, try to find decision makers and prepare the presentation mainly considering their profiles.

Define what your audience needs to know or do. Make confident recommendations based on your analysis, or lead the conversation toward the action that needs to be taken. Presenting possible "next steps" (statements starting with a verb) is an effective way to lead the conversation toward actions. An example might be "We need to invest more in this project since it has proved to be profitable for the company." It is also important to think about the possible opposition of the audience and analyze the facts or information that may be reported against your point.

Define the way you present the results. If we take the two extremes, on one side you have a live presentation where you are completely in control of the situation (you decide when and how people receive what information) and you don't need too many details in the presentation, since you are there to give them in case they are asked. On the other side, you have a presentation or document sent by email. Here you have almost no control over when and how the audience will consume it. Besides, you need to include many more details to cover at least most of the possible questions that may arise. In the case of a face-to-face presentation,

---

90   Cole Nussbaumer Knaflic, *Storytelling With Data: A Data Visualization Guide for Business Professionals* (Hoboken, NJ: Wiley, 2015).

remember that the slides mustn't contain presentation notes, but the visual elements that support your speech. You should write your speech notes apart, repeat them out loud, and ideally, you should give a mock presentation to some colleague or friend. Useful details do not have to be included in the presentation you are going to show, but you can create another document that you will give to the attendees afterward.

Define the tone of the presentation. Maybe you are celebrating a success, or presenting a problem to push people to act against it. In any case, you will have to adapt your speech and presentation to the appropriate tone.

Define the available data you can use to show your point. This doesn't mean showing only the data that supports your point of view, but to show all the relevant data. Moreover, the audience may spot the holes in your story and ask you to clarify these points.

Storytelling

Stories are very powerful because your audience is already familiar with this structure; they can identify themselves with the hero, and stories keep their attention. This means that your idea will be better transmitted and they will remember it more.

Nancy Duarte wrote a great book[91] about how to make presentations that "resonate," which I strongly suggest you read (this book has several examples of great speeches and presentations). Here I will introduce some of the main concepts related to storytelling, which can be very useful when planning a presentation.

First, you have to remember that a presentation is not a report presented through a PowerPoint. Neither is it a story, where dramatization is the key. Presentations are a sort of midpoint where you alternate facts and storytelling to give information in an entertaining manner. The main principle of storytelling to include in your presentation is the creation of a desire, which you will explain how to fulfill. This desire comes from a situation of conflict or imbalance (how it is now) and the fulfillment (how it would be) can be achieved if the audience decides to cross a threshold, start the adventure to solve the situation, and get the reward for the risk taken. For the audience, this step means a change to which they may be very reluctant, so your presentation will be about mentoring and persuading your audience about why they should overcome this threshold.

This idea comes from myths and stories, mainly the Syd Field's paradigm of the three acts that form a story (beginning, middle, and end) and the hero's journey described by Carl Jung. In the beginning, you have the setup where the characters and the situation are introduced. In the middle, you have the dramatic action and the obstacles that complicate the life of the hero who decides to start an adventure to solve the situation. And in the end, the hero solves the situation and comes back to the ordinary world with new insights and capabilities.

---

91   Nancy Duarte, *Resonate: Present Visual Stories That Transform Audiences* (Hoboken, NJ: Wiley, 2010).

Translated into the presentation language, we have three phases and two turning points:

Beginning: You introduce yourself, make it clear that that the audience is your hero, and present a situation where everybody agrees or can agree. In this phase, you must connect with them using shared experiences, goals that you have in common, or similar qualifications. For this reason, it is very important that you get to know them even before you start your presentation. You should segment them not only by demographics, but also understanding their lifestyles, knowledge, motivations, desires, values, etc. (e.g., you can use surveys). In this first part, your goal is to create the larger common ground between you and them (see "Be a Negotiator"), first by finding the existing one, and then by enlarging it.

Call to adventure: This is the first turning point where you present the conflict, the gap between what it is and what it could be. What it could be represents the destination of the hero's journey and you should carefully define it. First of all, you have to define the "big idea" to persuade your audience to start the adventure. This idea is a complete sentence that clearly makes your unique point explaining what it is at stake. You have to convince them that the sacrifice they have to do to make a change is worthy of the reward that waits for them. Therefore, you have to clearly identify and state the sacrifice and risk they will incur before they even mention it. You also have to acknowledge that the change you ask them is both internal (change the manner of being) and external (change the manner of doing). Finally, you must clearly define the reward, which can concern security, saving time or money, a prize, a new or better relationship, or the achievement of a dream. This must create a tension that will urge your audience to start the adventure.

Middle: This is the central part of your presentation where you explain the main ideas and topics, where you make your point. Here it is important to keep the attention by creating contrast. You can achieve that by comparing what it is and what it would be, by going back and forth from analytical explanation and emotional parts, or by delivering the message in different ways (media, style, etc.).

Call to action: This is the second turning point and here you explain more specifically what you want your audience to do.

End: Here you usually highlight again what it could be and the next steps to be taken for the adventure.

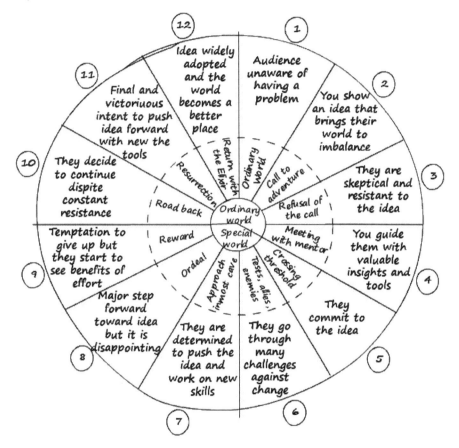

Figure 32: Audience's journey (Source: Adapted
from Nancy Duarte, Resonate)

Nancy Duarte suggests using a sparkline to plot your story. Sparklines allow you to define the chronological sequence, the different contrasts you are creating in the middle part, the "STAR" moments along with the presentation, and the main points.

I strongly suggest you read her book where you can find examples of sparklines applied to famous speeches, for example, Steve Job's launch of the iPhone. You can apply these principles to your speech. I wanted to show you an example using an entertaining speech about data and statistics: Hans Rosling's TED talks with the famous moving bubbles.[92] In his speech, he starts with an introduction, which is also a short story on his new job as a global development teacher to undergraduate Swedish students. *Stories* help to keep the interest of the audience and "humanize" the speaker; they bring him closer to the public. He then presents the current situation, or "what it is," the lower part of the sparkline. In this speech, the current situation is that people are quite ignorant about several global facts, such as mortality rates in different countries. He uses the examples of students and teachers taking a test about choosing the country with the highest mortality rate. Due to preconceived ideas, both students and teachers had poor results. This is the *shocking moment* when the problem becomes relevant and people start to feel the need to solve it. In addition, he makes this moment humorous by comparing the scores with hypothetical chimpanzees answering the questionnaire and getting better results than students and teachers. Then, Rosling explains that there is an urgent need to communicate in order to overcome preconceived wrong ideas.

At this point, in my opinion, we have the "star moment" when he contrasts the wrong idea of students about a world with two groups of countries (west and third world) using a chart with moving bubbles. The dynamic visualization, his exciting explanation of the moving bubbles, and the revealing new information that the audience receives—all this creates a sort of climax. At the end of the star moment, people see "what could be," that is, that the power of available data revealed by good *visualizations* can help overcome preconceptions and have a more accurate understanding of the world. During the rest of the presentation, he continues to create contrast with wrong preconceptions and the reality using

92   https://www.ted.com/talks/hans_rosling_shows_the_best_stats_you_ve_ever_seen

dynamic data visualizations. Moving the speech from what it is and what could be creates the necessary contrast to keep people interested and to make them think about it even after the presentation. Toward the end, Rosling talks about the *call to action*, namely the Gapminder project, how it works, and how it could change the world. And it is this very idea about how this project can change the world that has to be repeated at the very end of the speech to give a *"new bliss"*: a world with more knowledge-able people able to make better decisions.

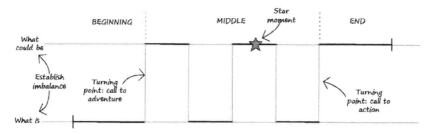

Figure 33: Speech sparkline (Source: Adapted
from Nancy Duarte, Resonate)

Be a Writer

Good writing is not only a nice-to-have skill, but it is essential to properly communicate the results of an analysis or to convince your boss about approving a certain project. Moreover, good writing makes you look like a better professional. To become an excellent writer, you need a lot of practice and dedication, but just applying some main fundamentals will make you a decent writer. To achieve this, focus on the organization of your document, its design, the writing style, and remember to carefully revise what you write.

Organization

The first step is to carefully organize your ideas in a logical structure. This is the backbone of your document that will make it not only easier to read, but will allow you to focus on writing instead of splitting your attention between organization and writing.

Besides the specificities of different types of documents, they all share a common basic structure: introduction, body, and conclusion.

Start with an *introduction* where you clearly state the purpose of the document. The purpose is the roadmap that will guide you toward your goal since it clearly defines what to include and what is not essential. All that you will talk about has to lead toward this goal. The purpose is followed by a description of your writing and the summary of your main points in order of priority. To define these points, it is a good practice to make a list of different ideas that lead toward your purpose, and then revise all the points, group them if they state the same or similar idea, eliminate points unrelated with your purpose, and order them by priority. Three is a good number of main points, but in case you clearly have two, four, or more points, you can use a different number. However, keep in mind that the more points you add, the more difficult it will be for the reader to assimilate them.

The next part of the document is the *body*. For each of the main points, sketch several supporting sub-points. The same process of grouping, cleaning, sorting that you did before has to be applied here. The next step is to develop these points, working on one paragraph at the time, each of which should contain only one main idea. Start each paragraph with a topic sentence, highlighting the beginning using bold format to orientate the reader. This topic sentence has to clearly and strongly define the purpose of the main point and it is what will guide you for the following content. As in the introduction, you have to order the sub-points by their importance.

Finally, you need a *conclusion* that simply concludes by summarizing your main points. Avoid the temptation of adding new outstanding information at the end, since it won't be effective if you haven't presented it at the beginning of your writing.

When you have larger documents than the basic structure presented here, you have to just follow the same process by multiplying this basic structure (introduction, body, and conclusion) for each of the sections, and by adding a global introduction and conclusion. Have a look at box 13 for an example of the structure of a short report concerning a study on revenue optimization of the two travel classes for a transportation company. This is about persuading your audience about the actions to be taken. If your document is not about persuading someone (i.e., it is informative), the main points will be different informative sections.

> **Box 13: Example of Short Report**
> **The purpose of this report is to identify the most important actions to improve revenues through a better price discrimination between the two travel classes.** Results show that our company can achieve a significant increase in revenues by improving coherence between the pricing strategies of the two classes, by revising their price gap, and by adopting ad-hoc tactics in case of second class saturation.
>
> 1. **Pricing strategies of the two classes must be coherent to avoid inefficiencies.** At present, the price of each class varies only according to its own level of demand and it creates inefficiencies, including sometimes having the price of the first class below that of the second class.
> 2. **Price gaps between them must be adjusted according to customers' price sensitivity.** The analysis of price elasticity shows that we can improve profitability by increasing the prices of the first class in long-haul tickets.
> 3. **In case of second-class saturation, first-class prices can be lowered until the prices of the second class.** When the demand forecast shows a possible saturation of second-class

seats, aggressive price reduction in the first class will increase both the number of passengers and revenues.

4. **The results of implementing these three actions have been statistically proved and we are confident they will increase total revenues by 10%.**

Design

Design is responsible for the first impression your document will generate to the reader. The content of the document will be better perceived if it gives an idea of order, good structure, and good aesthetic. The elements for good design are:

- Leave enough white space around paragraphs and other elements.
- Align paragraphs and other visual elements vertically and horizontally to give an idea of order.
- Don't use center alignment for text; use justified alignment or left alignment.
- Create short paragraphs—as a general rule no more than five lines.
- Use bullet points, bold text, subheads, and other elements to guide the reader through the document and to give an idea of a good organization.
- Use aesthetically appealing, but above all readable, typefaces (e.g., Arial).

STYLE

The style of your writing has to pursue clarity and brevity. Don't make your reader waste time with meaningless content or by writing unclear messages. When you write the first draft, don't worry too much about this. Just focus on properly defining and organizing your ideas. In the next drafts, you will start to pay attention to style:

- Use short sentences, if the length exceeds two lines, consider splitting the sentence.
- Be brief; as a rule of thumb, you should shrink your first draft from a third to a half for the final version.
- Cut as many useless sentences and words as you can.

- o Cut those that repeat the same concept (This will change customers' price sensitivity ~~and the way they perceive our prices~~").
- o Cut useless adjectives and adverbs ("This ~~interesting~~ study").
- o Cut qualifiers ("This is ~~really~~ efficient").
- o Cut "generalizers" (In general, everyone, always, never . . .).
- Be specific by clearly stating what you want to say without using expressions of doubt (maybe, possibly, I think . . .) and by avoiding general adjectives (use "The campaign increased sales by 20%" instead of "The campaign was very successful").
- Avoid jargon and replace it with something your audience can easily understand.
- Use active voice instead of passive voice.
- Limit the use of the verbs "to be" and "to have" by replacing them with alternative verbs or by paraphrasing your sentences.
- Limit the use of prepositional phrases by paraphrasing (use "She caught the morning train" instead of "She caught the train in the morning").
- Avoid repeating the same word or group of words many times.
- Be careful when you use modifiers ("The <u>recommendation</u> <u>that</u> <u>we implemented</u> was a part of the company's business plan" vs. "The recommendation was a part of the company's <u>business</u> <u>plan</u> <u>that was implemented</u>") and pronouns (it, he, she, they . . .) since they refer to the nearest preceding element; therefore, you should position them properly.

REVISION

You must revise your document several times and create several drafts. The first thing to revise is your structure. With so many versions and changes, you may have lost your original document structure. Then you should revise all your writing sentence by sentence and be sure they are as brief and clear as possible. Put yourself in your reader's shoes—they don't have your knowledge and don't know your context.

Be a Public Speaker

Public speaking is more challenging than writing, especially if you are not used to it or if you get nervous in such situations. However, a good speech is not only able to make your audience better understand your results, but it can also make them take action on your recommendations. Moreover, if you manage to deliver good speeches, you will appear to be a better professional, your analyses and results will look better, and you will significantly improve your reputation.

Delivering a good speech is challenging because on one side you have to adapt the content to the situation (audience, time limit, etc.) and you have to be extremely careful about the form of presenting results. While the content part (speech preparation) can be easily learned through theory and some practice, the speech delivery needs far more practice than theory since it involves the way you move, the words you use, the intonation of your voice, and so forth. Besides, you can be completely overwhelmed by emotions and you may lose control of your body.

In this chapter, I will demonstrate how to effectively prepare your speech, give you advice on how to deliver it, and finally some practical information on how to create great presentations.

Public Speaking

In the book *The Art of Public Speaking*,[93] Stephen Lucas describes the preparation of a speech as an effort in critical thinking since you have to logically organize and connect different ideas to lead your audience to a specific conclusion. Public speaking can be divided into two phases:

- Preparing the speech: In this phase, you analyze your audience, prepare and develop your topic, and organize your speech.
- Delivering the speech: After preparing and rehearsing your speech, it's time to deliver it in a relaxed and confident way to communicate your message.

PREPARING THE SPEECH
Analyze audience and setting
The message you want to deliver is filtered by the frame of reference of each listener and is affected by context. Therefore, before writing your speech, you have to analyze both your audience and the setting. You have to inform yourself about your audience concerning their demographics (age, location, occupation, etc.) and psychographics (opinions, attitudes, interests, background, etc.). It is quite important for you to understand the attitude toward your topic since you can put more effort in persuading the audience if they have an adverse attitude or put more effort in information if they are quite favorable to the topic. Sometimes, this information is not easily available, and you may plan to send a survey to the participants. It's a good practice to mix open, scale, and fixed questions in it.

Additionally, before preparing your speech and visual support, you need to know the characteristics of the room: its size, from where you will be speaking, whether you will have to use a microphone, the size of the screen for your presentation, whether you will have a podium where to put the laptop and your notes, and so forth.

---

93   Stephen E. Lucas, *The Art of Public Speaking* (New York: McGraw-Hill, 2007).

Purpose (inform, persuade, methods of persuasion)

In general, the two main purposes an analyst could have for a speech are either to *inform* or to *persuade*. For example, you may have to inform about the results of the previous year to the directors of your company, or you may have to convince the sales department that demand is inelastic and your company will make more profits by increasing prices. In either case, your purpose needs to be clearly stated in a sentence and then you have to commit to it when you develop your speech. After stating your purpose, take a moment to reflect on whether it is appropriate, whether you have enough time to accomplish it, and whether it is relevant for your audience. The next step is to develop your purpose into your central idea, usually including the main points of your presentation that support your purpose ("We can increase sales by 10% if we increase prices by 15% as it is proved by the statistical analysis and the experiments we have made"). As you can see in the example, the central idea should also clearly state what you are going to achieve.

Informing is relatively easier since you have to focus mainly on creating a good structure and on clearly explaining each point. To create a good structure, think carefully at the order of the points. Do it logically and whenever possible use the rule of "three"—namely three main points, each one with three sub-points, and so forth (highly recommended when you explain concepts in a topical order). In certain cases, you may choose a different order, for example, a chronological order when you have to explain several steps of a process.

When you speak to persuade, your goal is to influence the audience's opinion in favor of your point of view. You can have different degrees of persuasion, ranging from making the audience's opinion less opposed to yours to making your audience more in favor. The formulation of your speech will depend on the starting point of view of your audience.

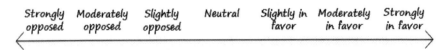

Figure 34: Degrees of persuasion (Source: Adapted from Stephen Lucas, The Art of Public Speaking)

We can identify three degrees of persuasion. In the first one, you just present one or more facts in a way to support your viewpoint. In the second one, the facts establish a standard that you will use in a second phase to express a judgment. In the third one, you specify the action to be taken, by establishing first a need, then presenting a plan, and finally explaining that the plan will work. Several structures can be used to organize the content, for example:

- Problem – solution
- Problem – cause – solution
- Competitive advantage (you compare the results with and without the action)
- Attention – need – satisfaction – visualization – action (Monroe's motivated sequence)

Let's revisit the example of the report presented in the chapter "Be a Writer." Imagine you have to prepare a speech for the company director and other managers to persuade them of the importance of applying those actions. If you were to use Monroe's sequence, your speech may be organized as follows:

- Attention: "Yesterday I was checking at our princes on our website and here you have what I've seen: 1st class 79€, 2nd class 89€ . . ." This is an example of how to get their attention, preferably when you support it with a striking visual.
- Need: "During the last year we have lost XXXX € because of the inefficiencies of our current price discrimination between first and second class. Every day we are losing XX€." This creates not only a sense of need to revert the situation, but also a sense of urgency to change it as soon as possible since every day we are losing something.

- Satisfaction: "We can solve this by implementing three single actions: 1) . . . 2) . . . 3) . . ." Here you explain how to solve the problem—how to satisfy the need introduced previously.
- Visualization: "Calculations and statistical analysis are robust and show a potential increase in total revenues by more than 5%." Here your audience visualizes that the solution is feasible and what they can obtain implementing those three actions.
- Action: "We need your help to properly implement these actions. I would like to ask you to . . ." Here you have to clearly say what you want them to do.

A persuasive speech uses several methods to persuade the audience:

- Credibility: The audience will already have prejudices, but during the speech you can improve them by showing your competence (show expertise and knowledge by talking about your background, the methodology you used, how you investigated) and your character (show that you are sincere and trustworthy). Good practices that improve credibility are to create common ground with the ideas of your audience, and talking moderately fast using vocal variety.
- Evidence: You can use examples, statistics, or testimony to support your point. Your evidence should be specific, from credible sources, and novel. Use reasoning to support your evidence and to reach a robust conclusion ("We have analyzed the prices available to customers during the last three months. We discovered that 10% of all transactions have a price for the first class equal to or lower than the price of the second class. This means that we are losing money in 10% of the transactions where we could have sold our first class at a higher price").
- Reasoning: With reasoning, you logically guide your audience to a specific conclusion. There are four main types of reasoning you can use:

- o Inductive reasoning: You use the results of several facts to draw a general conclusion ("We have several cases of first-class prices below second-class ones and several days where one of the two classes is completely full and the other one is empty. With this evidence, we can clearly understand that our pricing policy is not the most efficient").
- o Deductive: You use a general rule to draw the conclusion of a specific fact ("Our customers are not very price sensitive so a slight increase in price will have a positive effect on our revenues").
- o Causal: You explain an effect with a possible cause ("The performance of our first class started to decline just after implementing a new pricing strategy two years ago . . .").
- o Analogical: You apply the conclusion of a similar case to another one ("Last year we optimized the prices of our non-refundable tariffs and we had a very positive effect on revenues. We believe that we have a similar opportunity in the pricing strategy of our two travel classes").
- Emotions: Logic may not be enough to persuade, you have to accompany it with emotions. Emotions should grow naturally from your conviction, sincerity, and passionate delivery. In any case, you can stimulate them by using vivid examples and using an emotional language, but be careful not to exaggerate.

Support your ideas
You have four kinds of elements to support your ideas:

- Examples:
  - o Several brief examples to reinforce one idea
  - o One vivid extended example
  - o A hypothetical example
- Statistics: Use them sparingly, meaningfully, and from reliable sources. They can be used either to strengthen a point or to give

the idea of its magnitude ("every day we are losing € 1,000"; "this represents X% of . . ."; "the construction is as large as X football fields").

- Testimony: If you use testimony, remember to correctly quote or paraphrase.
- Citing sources: Use qualified and reliable sources; if necessary explain why these sources are credible. Give enough information to let the audience get the source.

Organize the beginning, body, ending

Introduction

The introduction is critical because you have to connect with your audience and create a sort of community. Start by welcoming your audience, thanking them for coming. Then you can introduce yourself and explain why you are giving the speech. You should also make acknowledgments if appropriate, but be careful to correctly say names and titles.

During the introduction, you have four main objectives: getting the attention, revealing the topic, establishing credibility and goodwill, and previewing the body.

First, to get the audience's attention, you have to relate the topic to them and explain why this is important for them. If they think the topic is not of their interest, they won't listen to you. You can also start with an intriguing statement or generating curiosity by not revealing all the details. Asking questions (both real and rhetorical) also helps to engage the public.

Second, you not only need to reveal the topic in a clear way, but you must also make the compelling point clear. The compelling point is the most important idea around which your speech is developed. It usually follows a brief context introduction and it is followed by the explanation of why it is important.

Third, make sure you have respect and credibility from your audience, if necessary by supplying information about your experience, knowledge, and education. In addition, the audience must believe in your goodwill. In case you think they doubt it, convince them of the contrary.

Finally, you must preview the body of your speech to prevent your listeners from guessing where you will lead them or getting lost during the speech.

Body

The structure of your speech is very important, if you don't have it clear, your audience will have it even less clear. A good practice is to create three main points that support your main idea, and drill down each point creating three sub-points. *Three* is a good number since it is not too much for a listener to remember and it is enough to support an argument. In this case, you are using a topical order and it is recommended above all in persuasive speeches. Another kind of order you may use in persuasive speeches is problem-solution, where you present one or more situation contraposing a problem with a solution to convince your audience about your point. If your speech is informative, you may choose a different order, for example chronological, spatial, or causal. You can take the example presented in "Be a Writer" where the main purpose is "to persuade our audience to optimize the present pricing strategy." Each of the three main points is then further developed in the speech, ideally, with the other three sub-points.

After defining and developing each point and sub-point, don't forget to link them with "idea connectors." These are elements that make your speech flow smoothly by linking two consecutive and nonconsecutive ideas of your speech. You have several options:

- A phrase that includes some elements of the previous idea and some elements of the new idea (e.g., "So far you have seen the problem, but let me present the solution"). An alternative is to use a specific keyword at the end of a point and retake it at the beginning of the next point.
- A brief preview of the next idea.

- A brief summary of the previous idea.
- Elements that represent the order (i.e., "first, second, third . . .").

Conclusion

It may seem obvious, but in the conclusion, you have to just conclude and not add something new. You again describe your compelling point, calling back to the beginning of the presentation, and therefore closing the loop. The audience must understand that you are about to conclude your speech, so you should modify your voice, pacing, and tone accordingly, as well as state you are concluding (e.g., "let me end by . . ." or "In conclusion . . ."). Use the conclusion to reinforce your idea by summarizing the main supportive points. End with something remarkable that your audience will remember and think about. You can use, for example, a dramatic statement or a quotation.

> **Box 14: Example of Conclusion**
> Today we have seen that the present pricing strategy creates important inefficiencies that produce a loss of potential revenues. To stop losing money, we have to carry out three actions as soon as possible: (1) improve the coherence between the pricing strategies of the two classes; (2) optimize their price gap; and (3) adopt ad-hoc tactics in case of second class saturation. Just today, we have lost 35,000€, and each day that we postpone these actions we'll be losing 35,000€. At the end of this month, we'll have lost more than 1M € . . . We have to act, and we have to act now.

Outlining

An outline is the blueprint for your speech. Basically, it is a scheme of your speech where you visualize your different points in a specific order and hierarchy. In the outline, you can add information such as transitions, clues for changes in voice or intonation, slides about related concepts, if you use a presentation, and so forth. This exercise is very useful to ensure you have a good and coherent structure and order as well as that your ideas are tied together and flow smoothly. A standard example is:

1. Introduction
2. Body
   a. Main point 1
   b. Main point 2
   c. Main point 3
3. Conclusion

You can also adapt it to the specificities of the situation and the topic, but avoid complicating it too much; otherwise, it will be more difficult for the audience to follow it. An example in an informative speech that a data analyst may face is:

1. Define the problem needing a solution.
2. Describe the hypothesis.
3. Describe the methodology:
   a. Detail 1 – data collection
   b. Detail 2 – data manipulation
   c. Detail 3 – analytical techniques and methods
4. Describe the main results:
   a. Detail 1 — chart
   b. Detail 2 — chart
   c. Detail 3 — table
5. Draw conclusions relating back to the problem and the hypothesis.
6. Suggest recommendations and future analyses.

The abovementioned outline is useful for the preparation part of the speech; however, during the speech you will need a shorter version to help you remember what to say. You should limit the text to keywords, short phrases, statistics, and quotations. It must be immediately visible, so use a legible font, abundant white space, and visual elements (color, font, symbols, etc.) that help you differentiate the elements (main points, sub-points, examples, quotations).

William Kuskin proposed an interesting example of speech outline in an MOOC (Massive Open Online Course) on Coursera about successful presentations.[94] Besides the introduction and conclusion that were already covered earlier, the interesting part is the modular body in which each module is composed of topic, data, and analysis. You first start your point, then you show some evidence that explains it, and finally, you make some analysis, assumptions, or conclusions. The most important thing is that the analysis section takes you to the first point, the topic. This becomes a circular concept and it must pivot around a main concept, represented by a keyword. In addition, this very keyword has to lead you to the next module in the smoothest possible way.

---

94   https://www.coursera.org/learn/presentation-skills/home/welcome

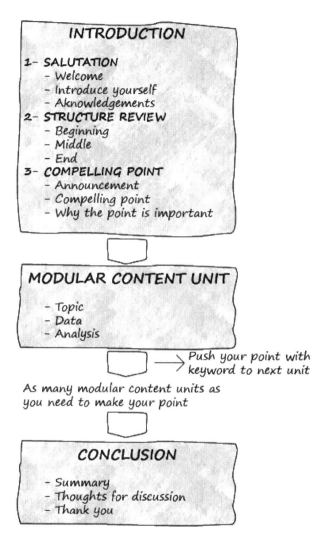

Figure 35: Speech structure (Source: Adapted from William
Kuskin, "Successful Presentations," Coursera)

DELIVERING THE SPEECH

Different approaches can be used for speech delivery—the only method
not really recommended is to read out your speech. You can either learn
it by heart or completely improvise. The problem with the first approach

is that it may seem unnatural and if you forget a small part, people will notice. The problem with the second approach is that it is more challenging to reproduce a well-structured speech, the ideas of which should stay connected and flow smoothly. Moreover, you may end up forgetting to say an important bit. A mixed approach that I find useful is to memorize just the structure with its keywords and some important short phrases. They are easier to memorize and they will bring to your mind the argument you planned to communicate. Bring with you the previously described outline (the speech outline) to help you remember statistics, keywords, and key phrases.

PRACTICING

If you are using the support of slides, don't put on them the script of your speech, since the audience has to pay attention to you and not read the text. Start by writing a script and rehearse out loud in front of a mirror. By rehearsing, you can detect excessively long points, sentences that are difficult to articulate, or parts where you stray too far from the concept you are trying to explain. Don't try to memorize it because you will not appear spontaneous; instead, try to interiorize it by memorizing several keywords that will lead you to the end of the presentation. Once you have interiorized it, put away your script and outline your speech from scratch on a new piece of paper (reverse outlining). This will both strengthen and organize your thoughts, and check whether the structure needs revision. You can also use this technique at the beginning when you are drafting your script, by outlining and reverse outlining it several times until your script reaches its final form.

In case of limited time, the one thing you absolutely want to rehearse is the introduction. It is critical to create a connection with your audience in the beginning:

- If you have a lesser number of participants, you can directly talk with them during the presentation; otherwise, try to come earlier and chat with some of them.

- Smile, put your chest forward, and be confident.
- End with passion when you talk about your compelling point; people will notice it and they will be more eager to be led by you.

When you practice your script, it's not only the words that matter, but also the tone and rhythm you use. You can directly sketch how to reproduce inflection points and rhythm on the outline used during the speech:

- Use bold font or underline letters that you may skip or that you want to pronounce more prominently.
- Use bold font or underline words that you want to emphasize.
- Mark rising and lowering inflections with arrows.
- Mark where you will make a pause.

This will avoid a monotone speech, and will help you to stress the most important points. Moving up and down your tone will create a rhythm that will help sustain your audience's attention.

In addition to the rhythm, rehearse your movements. They must be purposeful and appropriate. Start by defining a comfortable stance for you that may be either directly facing your audience, or standing with one foot slightly ahead of the other. Finding a comfortable and stable stance prevents you from body defense mechanisms under stress, such as moving your hands erratically, swinging, and so forth.

OVERCOMING FEAR

Public speaking can be quite a challenge, particularly if you are not used to it. Analysts may not be required to give great presentations, but if you aim to become a data artist, you will have to give good speeches and good presentations. The first step is to recognize the feeling of fear everybody experiences when they have to talk in public. You have to control it and transform it into positive energy, otherwise your body and brain will start to produce automatic defense mechanisms, such as losing the train of thought, using useless verbal fillers ("mmm," "like," "sort of"), sweating, swinging, or unnatural hand movements. To control this fear better, have a clear structure of your presentation and rehearse it several times. If you are confident about what you are going to say, then you can focus on your gestures, your voice, and your audience.

ENGAGING WITH YOUR AUDIENCE

I've already talked about the importance of connecting with the audience during the introduction, but I want to stress this point further. If you engage your audience from the beginning, if you create a strong community, you will prevent your audience from deviating their attention toward the many arising distractions (phones ringing, people walking out, side talks, etc.). Keep an eye on them during the speech in order to adapt what you are saying during the presentation. Look for signs of boredom or disagreement and try to correct your speech.

LANGUAGE

When you prepare the verbal part of your speech, don't just think about the meaning, but also about its form. The message must be clear so you should use simple, concrete, familiar, and concise words. For example, use "if" to "in the eventuality of" (simple), "hotels and bars" to "social locations" (concrete), "salt" to "sodium chloride" (familiar), or "Italians" to "people that live in Italy" (concise).

Make your language more vivid to *move* people instead of boring them. To do this, you can use:

- Imagery: similes (example), metaphors (example), or concrete words that recall smells, sounds, sights, etc.
- Rhythm:
  o Parallelism: "strong and weak"
  o Repetition: "If not now, when? If not us, who? If not together, how?"

o   Alliteration: "Improving the service is fundamental for our customers, but our customer's implication is not less essential for improving our service"

o   Antithesis: "Don't think about what your company can do for you, but what you can do for your company"

VOICE AND BODY

Voice is important to clearly transmit your message and engage the audience. Talk loud enough with good articulation and pronunciation for good delivery. Use a balanced speed (slightly fast when you want to move your public or to convey passion), avoid a monotone pitch that alternates up and down, and use pauses, for example, before an important keyword to create suspense.

Your body should move in harmony with your speech. Movements must be perceived as natural and spontaneous, and you have to give the impression of being calm (control any nervous twitches/movements).

DOES	Result	DON'TS	Result
Back straight, chest high, arms and chest open	You look confident and open	Cross your arms or legs	You look nervous, threatened and closed
Face the audience	You engage the audience	Turn your back to the audience	You lose the audience
Eye contact	People pay more attention and are more engaged	Avoid eye contact	People pay less attention and you seem insecure
Look at different people	Listeners feel they matter and pay more attention	Stare at a single spot	You seem insecure
Move during the presentation	You keep the attention	Stand in the same position	It seems you are afraid and may lose attention
Move according to your speech	It helps communicate your message	Move too much or fast purposelessly	You look nervous
Coordinate gesture with what you are saying	Your message will be stronger and you will get more attention	Repeat purposeless gestures and fidget	You look nervous and people pay attention at these movements instead of the speech

Figure 36: Do's and don'ts of body language for presentations (Source: Adapted from Soap[95])

Q&A

You have to properly manage the time for Q&A. Remember it is not about answering right or wrong, it is about reinforcing your relationship with the audience. Some recommendations are:

• Listen to the question carefully and ask the individual to repeat it if you haven't understood.

95 http://downloads.soappresentations.com/10_worst_body_language_presentation_mistakes

- Ask the speaker's name (if you don't know it) so you can address him or her directly.
- Start your answer by saying something like, "That's an interesting question."
- Take your time to think about the question, silently or out loud.
- If possible, try to connect ideas from different questions by remembering the keywords (and maybe also the names of the speakers).
- Adopt a soft tone to answer them, especially to harsh questions.
- But use a hard tone when a question that supports your point arises, exploiting it to reinforce your point.

Presentations

Following the principles of storytelling, you should organize the content of your presentation according to the three main parts of a story: beginning, middle, and end. The advantage of using the story structure is that your audience is already familiar with it. Therefore, they can devote all the effort to the content instead of trying to first understand the structure. Moreover, using storytelling ties together the different pieces of information and keeps the attention of the participants who are looking forward to what is happening next. This is the same principle used in novels, movies, or TV series.

Before starting, you must *get to know your audience*. Understand their background, their needs, what are the most important things for them. You may even have to create different versions of your presentation if you have to address different audiences. Knowing your audience will help you adapt both the presentation and your speech to the situation. For example, if your public is not at ease with numbers, you should dedicate more time and content space to explain graphs, ratios, calculations, etc.

After having gathered information about your audience, it is time to start outlining the main elements of the presentation. In the book *Beyond Bullet Points*,[96] Cliff Atkinson suggests using a *story template*[97] composed of different parts in a specific structure (see figure 37). Each part or box represents a slide and the phrase you write in it is its headline. Your *headlines* should:

- Be concise, complete, with a verb in an active voice, and with a maximum length of two lines when moved to the slides.

---

96   Cliff Atkinson, *Beyond Bullet Points: Using Microsoft© PowerPoint© to Create Presentations That Inform, Motivate, and Inspire* (Redmond, WA: Microsoft Press, 2011).
97   This structure is the one proposed in the book *Beyond Bullet Points*, but you can adapt it to better fit the situation. In the section "Public Speaking," I've proposed different alternatives that you can use.

- Be clear, direct, specific, and conversational to make the audience clearly understand them.
- Link the different ideas in the slides, for example, by using the same verb tense or by using similar sentence structures.

Remember that the few words that you put in theses slides are crucial, so you must get the writing right. You may get inspired by reading newspaper headlines or by taking the example of writers or poets who are able to condense elegantly a lot of meaningful information into a few words or sentences.

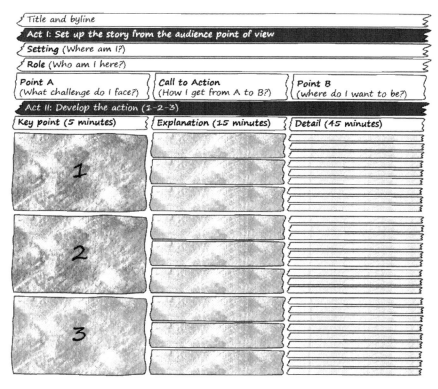

Figure 37: Speech structure (Source: Adapted from Cliff Atkinson, Beyond Bullet Points)

PLANNING THE FIRST FIVE SLIDES

The beginning of your "story" is an extremely important part because it determines whether you can engage your audience or not. Take the first part of the story template explained earlier and start by writing the headline and byline. This is the title of your entire presentation and it is important that you add a byline, namely the author, to improve the credibility of the information presented. Then, you have to define the headlines for your first five slides, which represent your story thread:[98]

Setting: Your first slide will inform your audience about where and when the story is set (e.g., "Across the industry, today . . ."). You can add extra information about the general situation, for example, ". . . returns are declining." This should be an element that puts everybody in the same starting situation, and it should be a point everybody can agree with it.

Role: The main character is your audience, make sure they get it ("You are looking for solutions").

Point A: This is the challenge that arises from a change (a new competitor enters the market, there's an economic shift, etc.). It represents a threat and/or an opportunity ("Your returns will stay flat if you do nothing"). Here you have to create the need for your audience to act, to engage with your presentation. Connect emotionally with them by using some of the principles explained in the chapter "Understand the Human Mind." For example, present opportunities as potential losses instead of potential gains. As you remember, we value more losses than gains.

Point B: This is where your audience wants to be instead of staying in point A. You should generate the desire to move to this point by creating a sort of tension ("You want your returns to improve").

Call to Action: This is the purpose of your presentation and the key point you should also visually highlight in your presentation (e.g., with a darker slide background). It can be explicit like "Hire us to help you find the returns you seek," but you can also make it less explicit using different

---

98   The information about presentations in this section is mainly based on the book *Beyond Bullet Points* by Cliff Atkinson.

verbs, namely "join us." In any case, this statement should be crystal-clear to leave no doubt about the call to action.

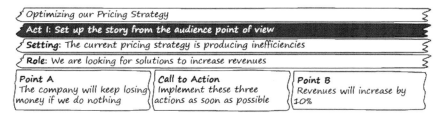

Figure 38: Example of Act I

To increase the efficiency of the audience's working memory, add a recurring theme (motif) throughout your presentation. You have to choose a structure familiar to your audience, even better if it can resonate[99] with them. Don't be afraid to be a little creative but remember to keep it simple. This creates a pattern that they can follow without wasting processing power of their working memory because its structure is already stored in it. It is also recommended to use an extendable motif, for example, a puzzle or a checklist that will more easily adapt to modifications. Other examples may be using a journey motif, a game motif, or a project motif. This pattern should be defined in the Call to Action, for example by making it clear for the audience that they have to complete the three-piece puzzle to find a solution.

---

99   In *Beyond Bullet Points*, the author presents the example of a presentation used in a trial where the motif was a CSI, where the audience had to identify the motive and means to prove the murder. This is an example of a motif that resonates with the audience and the presenter.

> **Box 15: Box Story Types**
> Examples of stories you can use to create the need to take action from the book *Beyond Bullet Points* by Cliff Atkinson:
> **Historical narrative** *"We have a history that makes us proud, and we want to apply our high standards to the current situation."*
> **Crisis** *"We have to respond to the danger facing us."*
> **Disappointment** *"We made a decision based on the best information we had available, but now we know it wasn't the right decision, so we have to try something else."*
> **Opportunity** *"We know something now that we didn't know before, which presents us with a new possibility if we act."*
> **Crossroads** *"We've been doing fine on the path that we're on, but now we have a new choice and we have to decide which path to take."*
> **Challenge** *"Someone else has achieved something amazing—do we have it in us to do the same?"*
> **Blowing the whistle** *"Although it appears everything is going fine, we have a serious problem we need to fix."*
> **Adventure** *"We know that trying something new is a risk, but it's better to take a risk than to stay in a rut."*
> **Response to an order** *"We've been told we have to do this, so we're here to figure out how to make it happen."*
> **Revolution** *"We're on a path to disaster if we don't radically change what we're doing today."*
> **Evolution** *"If we don't keep up with the latest, we'll fall behind."*
> **The Great Dream** *"If we can only see our possibility, we can make it our reality."*

PLANNING THE REST OF YOUR SLIDES

After defining the first five slides, work on the message about the call to action. Since by now the number of slides and the information may be overwhelming, you need to carefully assign priorities by establishing a *hierarchy*. I suggest you recall the call to action and define[100] three key points. For each key point, define three *explanations*, and for each explanation, three *details*. Each new level explains the *why* or *how* of the previous level. Have a look at the figure 39. In this example, the key points explain why the audience has to hire us to implement those three actions.[101] To define this hierarchy, you can either start by the key points and work down the hierarchical structure, or you can start with several unstructured pieces of information and organize them.

In the specific case of a data artist, these categories could be:

- Key points: recommendations or conclusions
- Explanations: explanations or analysis
- Details: methodology, data, or facts

The definition of this hierarchy not only helps you eliminate less important information, but it also gives you the order of slides for your presentation. A good practice is to highlight this hierarchy by visually identifying each level, for example, using a specific background color for each one. The clearer the structure for your audience, the better. Be aware that the vertical order also matters, namely when you list your three key points you should order them according to their importance.

Besides a good and recognizable structure, you should use a *similar style for the different headlines*, at least at the same level. You may revise it by sketching the slides of the same level together with their headlines and visual elements (e.g., three key points together, three explanations

100 By "defining," I mean writing the headlines, one for each key point, explanation, and detail. Each headline will be the title of its respective slide.

101 Despite the 3-by-3 structure proposed in the story template, you can adapt it to your needs. The structure may be chronological, sequential, spatial, or based on the importance of the topics.

that explain the first key point together, etc.). You can also revise the style coherence by using the headlines in a full sentence (e.g., "The main reasons for you to follow the Call to Action are: key point 1, key point 2, and key point 3).

Another important element is the motif you introduced in the call to action that should be recalled at least in the key points. If reasonably extensible, you should use the chosen motif also for the lower levels. This will help your audience keep track of where you are and to see the story as a whole instead of fragmented pieces.

Finally, this structure is also useful in case the time for your presentation significantly changes. The full version is suitable for a presentation of approximately forty-five minutes (considering a minute per slide), but if you have only fifteen-twenty minutes, you should cut the entire last column (Details), maintaining the coherence of your presentation. And if you have just five minutes, also cut the middle column (Explanations).

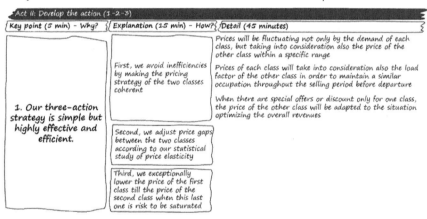

Figure 39: Example of Act II

SETTING UP YOUR STORYBOARD AND NARRATION

With your story template completed and printed, it's now time to import it into PowerPoint or Keynote. I suggest you use the template prepared by Cliff Atkinson,[102] but you can also do it manually by writing the

---

102 www.beyondbulletpoints.com

headlines in each slide. If you are not using his templates, in chapter 6 of *Beyond Bullet Points* you have some useful layout recommendations for headlines (Font: Calibri, 40, middle centered, vertically aligned, do not autofit, etc.). Also, remember that you have to use different backgrounds depending on the importance of the slides, for example, you can use different tonalities of grays. This will help you easily identify the structure of your presentation when you create it. Later, you can modify it if you think that another visual element can better convey the idea of hierarchy to the audience.

Print your slides to create your storyboard where you can sketch visual elements and write notes about the content. In the following example, the slides have been arranged in a hierarchical order, but you may choose a different arrangement for them. The important thing is that you need to have a complete view of your presentation and that you can work on it by hand.

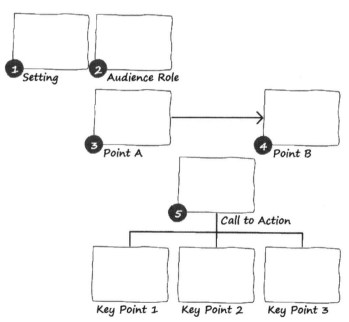

Figure 40: Storyboard sketchpad (Source: Adapted from Cliff Atkinson, Beyond Bullet Points)

Once you get your storyboard completed, open the Notes Page View of your PowerPoint and write your notes. Write in the notes section, not in the visual part of the slide. The main slide will only contain the title, visual elements, and eventually some keyword. Remember as a rule of thumb, you should talk for less than a minute per slide, so if the text is too much (if it doesn't fit in the available box, or by saying it loud), perhaps you should go back to the story template and create more headlines. This is a first draft, and you will probably modify it several times.

When you have filled all the notes spaces and you have a well-defined idea for each slide, you can start sketching the visual elements. When sketching, bear in mind three important rules:

- Simplicity: Use simple and clear illustrations so you avoid waste of energy for the working memory of your audience.
- Consistency: Visual elements must support the hierarchy of the slides. This means that you should use more memorable illustrations for the most important slides, while for other slides you can use more informative elements like charts, graphs, and so forth.
- Beyond the screen: Also consider other types of media elements, such as physical props or video clips. In the slide, you can just use an illustration that represents them.
- Use the power of stories: Recall personal stories and anecdotes to make a point that can connect emotionally with your audience. In addition, you can transform other information into stories, even data and statistics, by:[103]
  - Scaling: *WaterPartner.org's 2008 animation: "This year, 1 white girl will be kidnapped in Aruba, 4 will die in shark attacks, 79 will die of Avian flu, 965 will die in airplane crashes, 14,600 will lose their lives in armed conflict, 5,000,000 will die from water related disease. That's a tsunami twice a month or five Hurricane Katrinas each day, or a World Trade Center*

---

103 Duarte, *Resonate.*

disaster every four hours. Where are the headlines? Where is our outrage? Where is our humanity?"

o   Comparing: *Intel's CEO Paul Otellini's 2010 CES Presentation: "Today we have the industry's first-shipping 32- nanometer process technology. A 32-nanometer microprocessor is 5,000 times faster; its transistors are 100,000 times cheaper than the 4004 processor that we began with. With all respect to our friends in the auto industry, if their products had produced the same kind of innovation, cars today would go 470,000 miles per hour. They'd get 100,000 miles per gallon and they'd cost three cents. We believe that these advances in technology are bringing us into a new era of computing."*

o   Using context: For example, you can show the results of your company in different contexts.

To make your idea "resonate" more and make people talk about it after the presentation, you can plan one or few "STAR" moments (Something they'll always remember), which may be, according to Nancy Duarte, memorable dramatizations (props, demos), repeatable sound bites (repeating catchy phrases), evocative visuals, emotive storytelling, or shocking statistics. Remember the TED talk of Hans Rosling when he intensely presents the dynamic bubble chart. Another STAR moment was when Steve Jobs put the MacBook Air into an envelope in 2008 to show how thin it was.

SKETCHING YOUR STORYBOARD

The first slide to sketch is the one with the *title and the byline*. It should be intriguing since it is the first thing your audience will see, so you should choose an image that both reinforces the title and intrigues the audience. In our example, a magnifier glass can be a good visual representation for the title "Searching for Solutions." Here is also the place where you use the company's logo and (if appropriate) company's colors. Using the logo in the rest of the slides may be distracting and can create additional meanings you don't want to transmit.

Even if it was not planned, you may consider adding some *introductory slides*. The first one can be a slide about yourself to establish your authority by adding three images that represent who you are (e.g., your company's logo, a map of your country or region, and your favorite book or movie). A good practice is to animate these three images so that they appear sequentially. You can also add an additional introductory slide with a question mark where you ask your audience to introduce themselves (it depends on the kind of audience—if you know them there is no need to do that or if the audience is very large it may be impossible to do that with everyone).

Figure 41: Introductory slides (Source: Adapted from Cliff Atkinson, Beyond Bullet Points)

When you sketch these introductory slides, remember that they are critical to get the attention of the audience and to engage them, so you should use elements that engage emotionally.

In the *setting slide*, you may choose among several options to engage your audience. An option is to use a big picture of a magazine with an article that represents the current situation, for example, "Across the industry today, returns are declining." A second option is to narrate an anecdote blacking out the slide and surprising your audience, who would have expected some text or image. Another option is to show an impacting short video clip. But maybe these approaches are not the best way to engage a certain type of public, for example, a group of financial executives or analysts. In this case, you may represent a chart recognizable by everybody showing the increase of returns up to a certain point and then a decline of returns. If you are using a table, it is even more engaging if you draw the upward and downward parts of the line during the presentation to emphasize what you are saying.

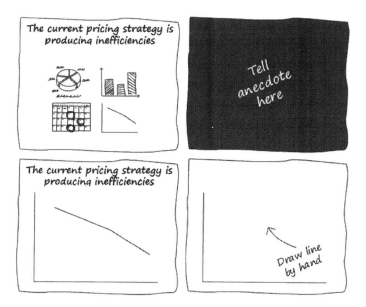

Figure 42: Setting slides (Source: Adapted from
Cliff Atkinson, Beyond Bullet Points)

The *role slide* should be linked to the previous one to keep the argument flowing. You can use the same image; by drawing something on it, you convey that your audience can improve the situation. If you use graphs, you may either add a line that improves the situation or you may use the image of the cover slide. In our example, I use a graph with increasing revenues. You can also simplify as much as possible, till the point of just including an image (see example in figure 43). At this point in the presentation, you may consider delivering a printed document with some more detailed data about the situation; however, be aware that it may distract your audience from what you are saying.

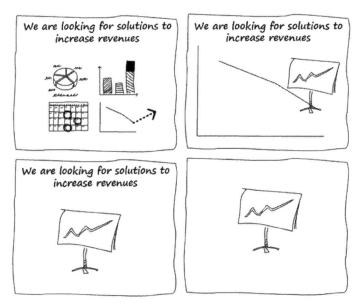

Figure 43: Role slides (Source: Adapted from
Cliff Atkinson, Beyond Bullet Points)

Slides of point A and point B must be sketched as a pair, for example showing in the first one a flat or downward line ("The company will keep losing money if we do nothing") and in the second one several dotted lines at the end of the flat line ("Revenues will increase by 10%"). Another option is to split the slide into two and add the point B part in the second slide (see the example in figure 44). Another option is to use a motif, for example, a checklist that is unchecked in point A and checked in point B.

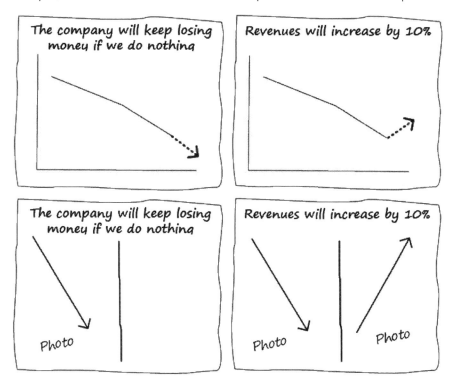

Figure 44: Point A and B slides (Source: Adapted from Cliff Atkinson, Beyond Bullet Points)

A good recommendation is to visually bond together these first slides to make your argument flow smoothly through them. In the example given in figure 45, the same graph is used in the setting, role, point A, point B, and call to action slides, while the magnifying glass and the company's logo in the title slide are recalled in the call to action slide, which is the one that summarizes the purpose of your presentation. Moreover, using animation makes your presentation more dynamic and better synchronized with your speech.

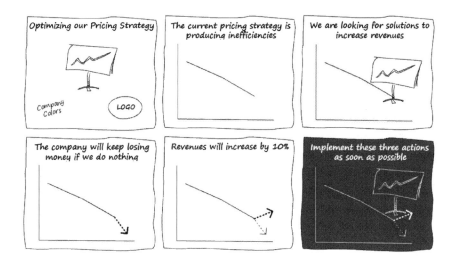

Figure 45: Act I slides (Source: Adapted from
Cliff Atkinson, Beyond Bullet Points)

Call to action (CTA) and key point slides are the most important parts
of your presentation. The CTA slide is an anticipation of the three key
points and you can recall them creating a tryptic with the three illustrations representing the three key points. However, in this slide, you won't
add any additional information about the key points, since you will explain
them properly in their respective slides. Showing or giving to the audience a physical prop at this point can increase the perceived importance
of these slides.

Figure 46: Key points slides (Source: Adapted from
Cliff Atkinson, Beyond Bullet Points)

Instead of simply showing three images, you can use a motif through-out the four slides, for example, a formula that is completed by the three key points or a puzzle made by three pieces (see figure 47). Notice that when you use a motif— the puzzle pieces for example—you are not show-ing only the new piece, but you are retaining the previous ones.

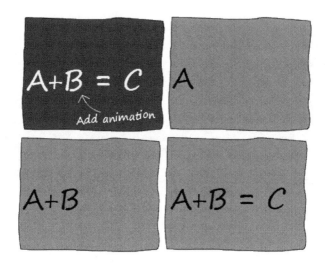

Figure 47: Key points using a formula (Source: Adapted from Cliff Atkinson, Beyond Bullet Points)

If visually adequate, you may also recall points A and B in the CTA slide (see figure 48).

Figure 48: Recalling points A and B in the CTA (Source: Adapted from Cliff Atkinson, Beyond Bullet Points)

To make the hierarchy and structure more perceivable, you can add two important elements: the layout and a navigation bar. In figure 49, you can see how to highlight the CTA slide and, with less intensity, the key point slides.

Figure 49: Example of using the layout to make people perceive the structure (Source: Adapted from Cliff Atkinson, Beyond Bullet Points)

A navigation bar can be very useful to make your audience keep track of where they are on the presentation, mainly in the explanation and detail slides due to their quantity. In this navigation bar, you should recall the key point associated with the explanation slide, or the key point and the explanation slide associated with the detail bar. If you are using a specific motif in the key point slides, you can use it for the navigation bar.

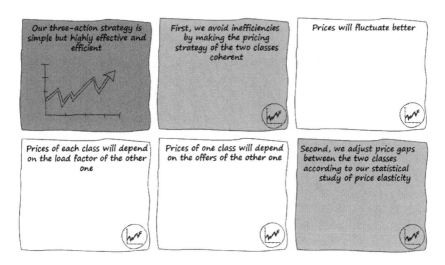

Figure 50: Example of using the navigation bar to make people perceive the structure (Source: Adapted from Cliff Atkinson, Beyond Bullet Points)

The main principles described so far can be applied to the *explanation slides*. Since they explain a key point, they should recall it, for example by using the abovementioned navigation bar. In addition, the three slides must be sketched together, maintaining a certain flow. They may be linked conceptually. For example, you can use a diagram that is completed through the slides (figure 51) or at least visually if the different explanations are not related (e.g., using a visual organizer like a checklist). Here you may also use screenshots to present a sample of something, for example, a part of the spreadsheet used for an analysis.

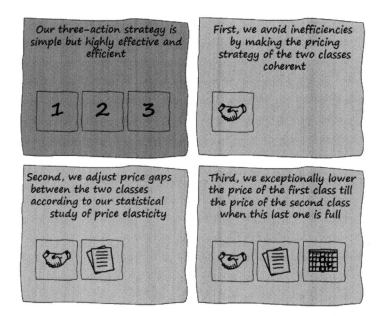

Figure 51: Example of conceptual linking (Source: Adapted from Cliff Atkinson, Beyond Bullet Points)

In the *detail slides*, you are showing detailed information and usually, you don't need to add motifs or recall the explanation slide systematically, since it may be too excessive. You may simply add a navigation bar if appropriate (it can just recall the key point; it may not be necessary to recall also the explanation slide). In these slides, you can consider using other media to present demos or show features of a product. In any case, remember to adapt them to your profession (in the case of an analyst, captures of the analytical tools, graphs, charts, diagrams, etc.).

For Act III (Conclusion), you can use the same slides of point A, point B, and CTA without headlines, since it is a good practice to end the presentation by recalling the present situation, and what your audience has to do to improve it.

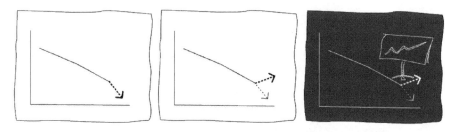

Figure 52: Example of Act III (Source: Adapted
from Cliff Atkinson, Beyond Bullet Points)

ADDING GRAPHICS TO YOUR STORYBOARD AND PRESENTING

When substituting the sketches with the real illustrations, you should keep in mind the following:

- Opt for the appropriate solution depending on the available time to finish the presentation and available budget.
- Illustrations should respect both the kind of audience and the general tone of the presentation (e.g., if the audience is quite formal, don't use cartoon-like images).
- Illustrations and the layout should form an aesthetically appealing whole (have a look at the principles explained in the next chapter concerning alignment, colors, etc.).
- Use animation to reinforce the sequence of information that your audience has to process, namely first the headline and then the graphic.
- A practical tip is to start by filling the slides with the illustrations you already have, followed by those that you can get easily, and finally completing the rest.

REHEARSAL, ENVIRONMENT, QUESTIONS, AND HANDOUTS

Rehearse your presentation in front of some colleagues or friends, where you also have to take care of your voice, intonation, and pauses. On one hand, you should show interest and enthusiasm in what you are presenting, and on the other hand, you should use nonverbal elements (intonation and pauses) to emphasize the most important points.

The environment is also very important. Make sure a big screen will be behind you, with appropriate light, and that you will have a sort of podium for your notebook from where you can read your notes. You may also adapt these notes to work as quick reminders of the main points you are going to talk about in each slide. It is a good practice to print these kinds of notes, as well as the entire presentation in case of any problem.

Finally, before presenting, you should consider two elements: questions and handouts. Plan carefully if you decide to ask for questions (or opinions) during a certain part of the presentation—for example, to confirm the key points, or at the end. In any case, make sure this doesn't steer away from the flow of your storyline. Handouts before the presentation are usually appreciated by the audience because they can take notes on them; however, they may distract. You should carefully consider the pros and cons, or you may try by delivering a handout without the notes before the presentation, and after, if needed, you may deliver the complete handout.

You can download useful templates of *Beyond Bullet Points* at www.beyondbulletpoints.com and interesting presentations templates at http://soappresentations.com/downloads/.

Be a Designer

A esthetics is perhaps too often overlooked in data analysis where the "important stuff" is the soundness of the model, the generation of insights, and the actions to be taken. I completely agree with that; however, taking care of the aesthetics significantly improves the effectiveness of communication of results. If you use pleasant colors, a well-organized distribution of graphs, adequate white spaces, good pictures, and so forth, you will catch your audience's attention and your results will look better. Several studies have shown that beautiful aesthetics make people perceive products easier to use and of better quality. The same psychological phenomenon will happen with the results you present. Make them beautiful so that your audience will perceive them better and will be more eager to adopt them.

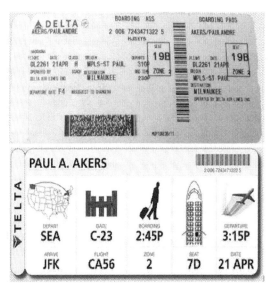

Figure 53: How good design can improve communication—
example of a plane ticket from Paul A. Akers

The first section of this chapter is about the basics of graphic design: how to organize the space, how to use different design elements (color, typefaces, pictures, and other graphic elements), and which techniques to use to improve the aesthetic appeal of visualizations. In the rest of this chapter, I will focus more on the specific design elements used by data analysis: data visuals (graphs, tables, etc.). After introducing the main types of data visuals, I'll explain some visualization principles to improve them, and I will conclude by reviewing some practical suggestions on how to create useful dashboards.

Graphic Design

The content of what you have to communicate is only a part of the message. It's the design and aesthetics that first impact your audience. A good design not only makes it easier for the message to pass through, but it also makes you look professional.

The first step to become a good designer is to look at many examples for inspiration and to create a personal archive with the visualization that you found more interesting. When you have to work on a specific design, try not to look for examples of the same kind, but try to search for different things to get the inspiration and to create something different. For example, if you have to create the cover of a presentation on the results of a market research, don't look for "Market research PowerPoint templates" but look for different kinds of visuals, for example, "National Geographic covers" and you may get an original idea for your presentation.

ORGANIZATION

Organization is very important in graphic design and you should start any project by defining a grid. A grid is made up of lines that on one side define spaces and, on the other side, make sure everything is aligned. Alignment is key to create harmony and convey professionalism. When you create your grid, pay special attention to the negative space, the space that will be left blank. You should have enough white space to visually separate your elements and to lighten the design.

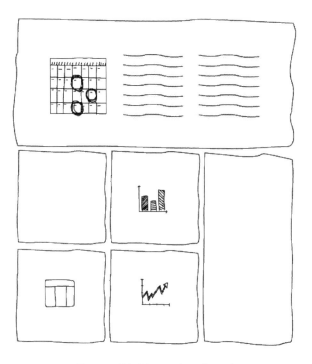

Figure 54: Example of grid

When deciding where to place your most important element (or elements), consider the rule of thirds, according to which the most visible parts are the intersection of the lines that divide the space into nine rectangles (figure 55). In particular, the upper-right intersection is naturally visualized first when people are scanning an illustration, a page, or a slide. You can also use many other techniques to draw attention toward the main element such as contrast. Remember also to place a title or the most important element above the center, and not exactly on the center since it is perceived as more natural. Look for example at book covers.

Figure 55: Rule of thirds

Finally, if you don't have strong reasons to use specific proportions, you may use the golden ratio: approximately 1.6. This is a ratio that is present in nature and that it has been used in many paintings and designs. It creates a natural-looking composition, making it aesthetically pleasing for your audience. You can use it to define the ratio between a title and the text in the body, the size of a sidebar in a webpage, or the ratio among different images of different sizes.

Figure 56: Example of the golden ratio

ELEMENTS

The elements you can play with in a composition are typefaces, colors, images, and graphics.

Typefaces play a very important but often undervalued role in composition. They must be appropriate for the message you communicate and can also be used as a design element, as you can see in the following examples. The one on the left is a "nested title," which is often used on book covers; the one in the middle concerns the use of the first capital letter of a paragraph as a design element; the one on the right shows the use of size and color of the text to create a specific design.

Figure 57: Role of typefaces in composition

A best practice is to combine two typefaces, one serif (e.g., Times New Roman, Baskerville, Garamond) and one sans serif (Arial, Helvetica, Verdana). Usually, the sans serif typeface is used for the title while the serif one is used for the body. However, I find it very clean and modern to use sans serif for the body, as you can see in this book or in other books quoted here such as *Storytelling with Data* and *Resonate*. The important thing is not to use typefaces of the same family (e.g., using two sans serif together, namely Arial for the header and Verdana for the body) since it creates an unpleasant effect. In addition, don't use just the typeface to differentiate header and body; use also size and weight (bold vs. normal).

Lowercase must be preferred to uppercase when the amount of text is larger than a name, a title, or a very short sentence. The reason is that we not only recognize words by reading the letters, but also by their shape. Therefore, using uppercase, we level all the letters, lose the shape of words, and make them more difficult to read. However, when the amount of text is limited, uppercase text can be used as a design element that contrasts with lowercase text.

ant ANT

Figure 58: Lowercase versus uppercase

Concerning *alignment*, the left one is the easiest to read and so it must be preferred for the body of a document. You can also make the layout more attractive by using justified text, but it is better to avoid it on narrow columns due to the white spaces it creates between certain words. Centered text should be used only for titles, headers, or captions, while the right alignment must be used only in limited circumstances (if you have to align a small amount of text to a picture on its right). Right alignment is also useful in tables if you have categories in the first column and you want to make them visually closer to the figures on the second column.

THE USE OF ALIGNMENT

Concerning alignment, the left one is the easiest to read and so it must be preferred for the body of a document. You can also make the layout more attractive by using justified text...	Concerning alignment, the left one is the easiest to read and so it must be preferred for the body of a document. You can also make the layout more attractive by using justified text...	Concerning alignment, the left one is the easiest to read and so it must be preferred for the body of a document. You can also make the layout more attractive by using justified text...	Concerning alignment, the left one is the easiest to read and so it must be preferred for the body of a document. You can also make the layout more attractive by using justified text... 

Figure 59: Different types of alignment

Finally, remember that whatever typeface you use, the text must be easily readable—with an adequate size and an adequate weight and color to create a sufficient contrast with the background. If you have different colors in the background (e.g., a picture), use borders, shading, or a translucent background to make the text easily readable.

Color is another powerful element to be used carefully in your compositions. First, bear in mind that different colors convey different feelings. Green transmits safety, fertility, growth, while red transmits energy, danger, and passion. Blue, on the other end, symbolizes wisdom and safety, and you may notice that it is used by several financial and insurance companies in their logos.

Besides the feelings evocated by different colors, the main recommendation is to use them naturally, that is, emulate nature. For example, in nature, you usually don't find subdued colors (red, yellow, blue) but you find more pastel colors, with less brightness and less saturation. If you look at the palette of whichever application, you will notice that the fully saturated colors don't look very natural, and you should prefer less saturated ones, namely from 70% to 40%. The less saturation you use, the more easily you can combine different hues (what we commonly call colors such as green, brown, etc.). If you use pictures in your presentation or document, a good trick is to pick one of its colors and use it for other visual elements.

Finally, you may consider using *pictures* and *graphic elements* in your compositions, and they have to be in harmony with the rest of the elements. For example, don't take pictures just the way they are, but adjust their contrast, brightness, and so forth, to make them more suitable for the context. You may also use sublimation (use a colored background such as black, white, or blue and make them transparent) or make them black and white. Among graphic elements, there are those specifically used to visualize data: numbers, table, and graphs. These elements will be covered in the sections about data visualization.

TECHNIQUES

There are some useful techniques you should consider to make your compositions more aesthetically appealing.

Contrast makes visualizations far more interesting for your audience. This technique can be applied to pictures, documents, or mixed compositions and can be created by different elements: brightness, shape (curved lines vs. ones with sharp angles), color (yellow on gray background), and scale.

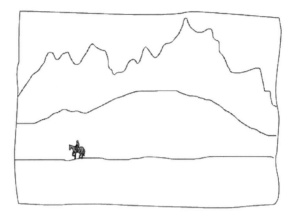

Figure 60: Example of contrast using size

The use of abundant *white space* (or empty space) conveys elegance and invites the audience to screen what you are proposing. Moreover, white space highlights the main message, making it easier for your audience to identify it.

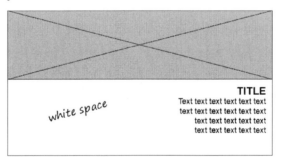

Figure 61: Example of abundant white space

Another technique is to create harmony and rhythm with *repetition.* For example, you can repeat a certain shape in order to create an aesthetically pleasing pattern. As an analyst, consider the importance of it in a document where you can use repetition also to make the audience easily identify specific elements (you can use a specific color to identify specific elements such as informative boxes, recommendations, etc.).

Figure 62: Example of repetition

Sublimation, which I've mentioned before concerning the use of pictures, is a good technique to boost the potential of pictures. You can play with different sublimations to create contrast between the two areas.

Overlapping different graphic elements is useful to create more stability by linking them together.

Figure 63: Example of overlapping

Finally, remember that the audience must easily identify a *clear target* and follow other elements according to the priority you gave them. The natural scanning process of the eye is from left to right and top-down, so respect this principle when deciding the positioning of visual elements. Besides using the different elements and techniques described so far (color, contrast, position, scale, white space, etc.), you can create a sort of *tension and movement* in the composition by:

- Putting items closer.
- Move items to the border of the available space or even cutting them.[104]
- Tilt graphic elements or text.
- Unbalance elements by moving them out of the center.
- Use sharp angles.

---

104 Creative cropping is a widely used technique to create a sense of movement and to awaken the curiosity and imagination of the audience since you hide an interesting part of a picture.

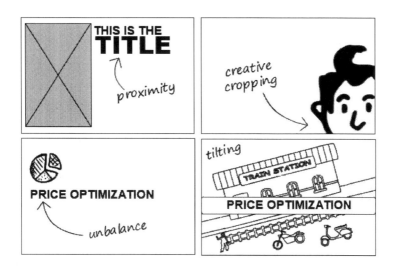

Figure 64: Examples of tension and movement in graphic design

Data Visualization

Whether you will use a presentation, a document, or a dashboard, charts are probably the most important elements in your communication. They are far more powerful than numbers and text to persuade or inform your audience. As Scott Berinato suggested,[105] making good charts requires you to adopt "visual thinking." Adopting visual thinking means understanding how we see and interpret visual elements. First, we don't follow a specific order like in reading a text. Of course, we tend to start by looking at the upper-left corner, but our eyes go where visual elements stand out (bold text, highlighted elements, peaks and valleys in graphs, intersections, outliers, striking colors). Look at the chart in Figure 65 and notice that your attention is caught by the intersection of the two lines. You will probably read the lines labels, and without even reading titles, subtitles, or the axes, you get the idea that the urban population has outnumbered rural one. Many effective charts show a single important point.

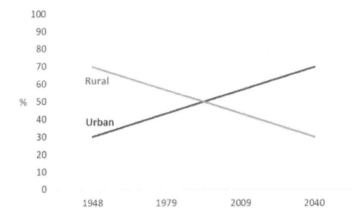

Figure 65: Example of chart with a single important point
(Source: Adapted from Scott Berinato, Good Charts)

---

105 Scott Berinato, *Good Charts: The HBR Guide to Making Smarter, More Persuasive Data Visualizations* (Boston, MA: Harvard Business Review Press, 2016).

Second, we can only see a limited number of visual elements at once. As a rule of thumb, starting with five to ten elements, we are no longer able to clearly identify individual elements, but we start to see global or average patterns. If on one side this implies that you have to limit categories, on the other side you can exploit this fact to make your audience see global patterns by showing many individual elements, as you can see in the example in figure 66. In the first graph, the performance of individual workers creates a general upward trend that can be more insightful than just showing the average trend variation of all workers. In the graph on the right, the global trend is moved to the background to highlight the performance of the top workers. This allows to see both team performance and the most important individual performance variations.

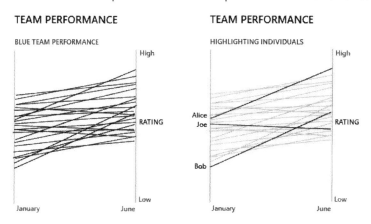

Figure 66: Example of global trend versus individual trends in a line chart (Source: Adapted from Scott Berinato, Good Charts)

Third, we always try to seek meaning, identify patterns, and make conclusions of what we see. Therefore, you have to carefully use colors, names, and positions because you may unintentionally create misleading associations, trends, or patterns. For example, when you show a trend in time, the choice of the time frame can completely change the message you show.

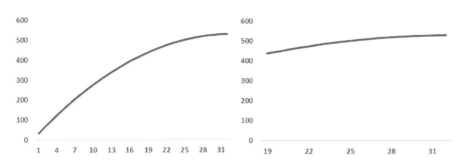

Figure 67: Example of the different meaning you can convey choosing a different time frame

Finally, remember that we expect that charts respect some conventions. For example, you expect to see time on the horizontal axis and that it chronologically goes from left to right. Other examples are that upward means increase in value, while downward means decrease in value. If you break these conventions, your audience will be misled and they will need extra time and effort to correctly read your chart.

In data visualization, you must take into consideration both the context and the design execution. Since I've already introduced the concept of context, in this section I will focus on the design execution which must respect two fundamental principles:

- Expressiveness: Communicate what you have to, no more, no less, and avoid misleading your audience.
- Effectiveness: Use the best available solution you have at your disposal.

Moreover, I will focus on what Scott Berinato calls "Everyday DataViz," namely data-driven charts used to declare a specific idea. The author identifies also other three types of charts: (1) data-driven charts whose goal is to explore or confirm possible hypotheses; (2) conceptual charts used to illustrate ideas; and (3) conceptual charts used to generate ideas. Examples of conceptual charts are flow charts, decision trees, or organization charts. If you want to know more about this subject I suggest you read the book *Good Charts*[103] and *Storytelling with Data*,[106] which were the main source of inspiration for this chapter.

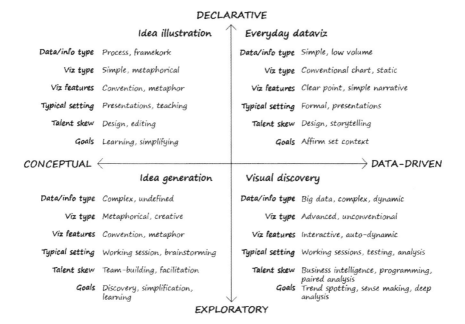

Figure 68: Types of charts (Source: Adapted from Scott Berinato, Good Charts)

---

106 Knaflic, *Storytelling with Data*.

CHOOSE THE BEST AVAILABLE SOLUTION

The first phase when building a chart is thinking about what you want to communicate. Of course, you will already have analyzed your data, but you should try to forget about it for a moment. Don't be limited by the constraints of your data. Also think about where, when, and to whom the chart will be presented. Talk to someone, the conversation can add additional information and can improve the message you want to communicate. It is important to clearly understand the reasons why you are going to create and present this chart.

In the second phase, you start sketching it, preferably on a paper. At this point, you are visualizing your chart and this means that you have thought about a specific kind of chart. To help you in this task, Scott Berinato suggests writing down what you want to show and taking notice of the keywords used. In his book *Good Charts*, he presents an interesting example: "I want to COMPARE THE NUMBER of job posting to hires to SEE what THE RATIO is for DIFFERENT TYPES of jobs." The keywords highlighted in this phrase suggest you use a chart to compare ratios of different categories.

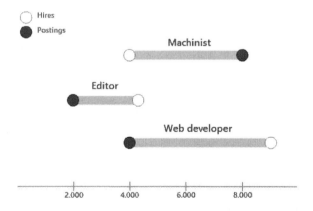

Figure 69: Example of chart comparing job hires and job postings
(Source: Adapted from Scott Berinato, Good Charts)

The author also suggests a very useful template you can use as guideline for choosing the most appropriate chart based on the keywords you identify in your phrase.

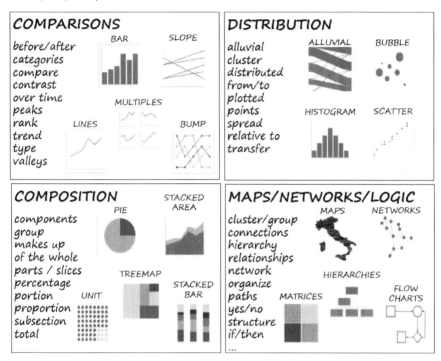

Figure 70: How to choose a type of chart based on keywords
(Source: Adapted from Scott Berinato, Good Charts)

As an additional source of inspiration, you can have a look at the "Chart Chooser" proposed by Dr. Abela in his blog www.extremepresentation.com and the Data Visualization Catalogue by Severino Ribecca (www.datavizcatalogue.com).

As I said, this is a good source of inspiration but of course, they are not exhaustive and you don't have to stick to them. It is useful to see different options and ways of visualizing data. You don't have to memorize all kinds of charts, but it is important to learn the basic types and then collect examples that you find interesting. In specific cases, you can also use hybrid solutions and innovate with the standard charts to better adapt them to the situation. But also remember that the more you complicate and deviate from "standard," the more difficult it will be for your audience to understand your charts. A complex solution must be used only when a simpler chart can't convey the message.

Finally, after sketching, you create your first (probably of several) prototype, which is a cleaner, more realistic version of your sketch. Depending on the quantity and complexity of data, you may either use real or realistic data, and you will probably use a design tool (Excel, Power BI, Tableau, Adobe Illustrator, etc.).

Sometimes, what you want to communicate does not have a perfect solution but remember the principle "choose the best available solution," which is not necessarily the perfect solution. Look at figure 71. Imagine you want to show the performance in different attributes of your company versus several competitors. In the first chart, you try to show the performance of all combinations of company/attribute, but it is quite difficult to read. Then you try to simplify it using bars and highlighting your company and its relative position in each attribute (second chart). This is a far more elegant solution that lets you clearly understand your company's performance in each attribute. However, you are losing part of the information, namely the performance of each competitor throughout each attribute. If this information is not important to you, you can stick to the bar chart; otherwise, you need to look for other solutions. You may add colors to the bar chart, but it is confusing and your company won't stand out anymore in the graph. Even if line charts should not be used with categorical data (attributes), an "ok" solution may be to use a line chart with a different line for each competitor in order to identify them throughout the different categories. In this case, it is important to directly label lines to facilitate the identification of each competitor.

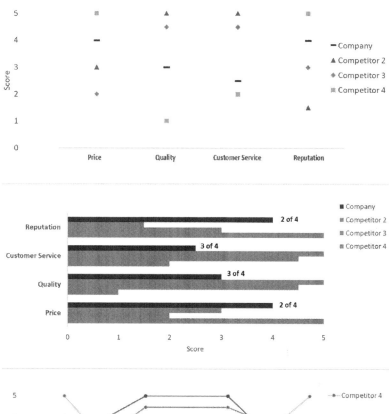

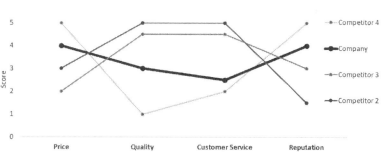

Figure 71: How to modify your chart to reach the best available solution

USE A CONSISTENT STRUCTURE AND VISUAL ORDER

If your chart is well structured and elements are well positioned, you improve both its readability and aesthetic. The advantages of an easier-to-understand chart are quite clear, but what about aesthetics? A "beautiful" graph has several advantages; for example, it grabs the attention of the audience, it is more effortless to read, it seems more professional, and conclusions are more convincing.

Start by applying a standard structure with a specific order and weight: title 12%, subtitle 8%, field 75%, and source line 5%. Obviously, you don't have to strictly stick to these proportions, but they are good guidelines from where to start. Then, depending on the specificities of the situation, you may need to modify them. For example, the kind of data may require a higher field to detect trends, or maybe you don't need a subtitle because the title and field are clear enough. Legend, if included, goes in the field part, usually on the right side or at the bottom. As a general rule, include axes, axes names, demarcations with values, and data values. I will later look at the removal of unnecessary and redundant elements. I usually start by including most of the elements and then I work backward removing the superfluous ones. I find it simpler to check them one by one and asking myself if they are useful to convey the idea.

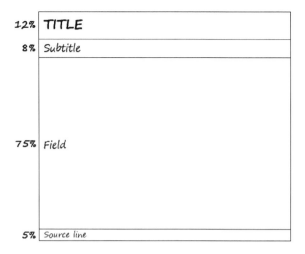

Figure 72: Chart structure (Source: Adapted
from Scott Berinato, Good Charts)

Finally, to improve the visual order of your chart it is advisable to respect:

- Alignment: Whenever possible, align vertically and horizontally the different elements (e.g., using a justified or flush-left text alignment); avoid diagonal elements since they look messy and the diagonal text is slower to read.
- White spaces: Don't fill every free space of your slide or page since it is uncomfortable, it generates stress, and it deviates the attention away from the important parts of your communication; leave enough empty space between objects, in margins, and use spaces strategically to highlight what it is really important (you may also present a single number in a blank page).

In figure 73, you should notice the improvements made on the second chart, namely (1) the respect of the standard structure, (2) the alignment of title, subtitle, and source line with the vertical axis, and (3) the use of abundant white space.

Alberto Scappini

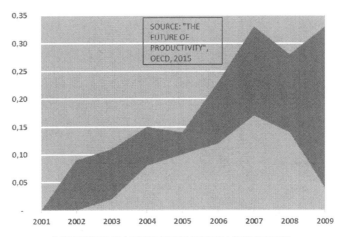

DIFFERENCE IN LABOR PRODUCTIVIY LEVELS FROM
THEIR 2001 VALUES FOR "FRONTIER FIRMS" AND
EVERYONE ELSE

THE GAP BETWEEN THE MOST PRODUCTIVE
FIRMS AND THE REST IS GROWING

Percentage difference in labor productivity levels from their 2001
values (index, 2001=0)

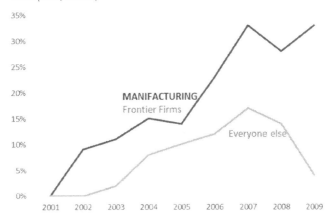

SOURCE: "THE FUTURE OF PRODUCTIVITY", OECD, 2015

Figure 73: Example about how to visually improve a chart
(Source: Adapted from Scott Berinato, Good Charts)

LEAD YOUR AUDIENCE TOWARD THE MAIN IDEA

As explained before, visualizations are not read in a specific order like texts. For this reason, you have to carefully plan how to highlight the important elements to make your audience understand the main idea you intend to communicate. Therefore, start by defining what you want to communicate. For example, in the following chart the main idea to be communicated is that non-mortgage debt is increasing much more than mortgage debt.

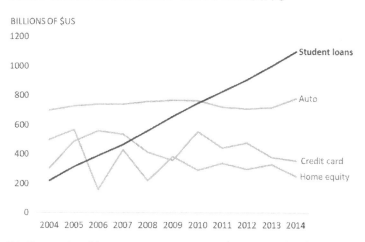

Figure 74: Example of how to communicate the main idea by highlighting the main line (Source: Adapted from Scott Berinato, Good Charts)

The key elements you can work with to lead your audience toward the main idea are contrast, positioning, and additional elements. *Contrast* works well when we have a few types of elements of contrast to compare (ideally two colors, two shapes, etc.). It is easier to spot a blue element among many gray ones, but it is more difficult to spot it among many different colors. In the example in figure 75, the performance of our company and several competitors are compared. However, while in the first graph it is quite complicated to identify how our company is performing in the different attributes, in the second graph we clearly get it. Besides contrast, *positioning* has been used in the example since the attributes are presented in descending order starting from our company's performance. The audience will start looking at the graph by the upper-left element. In this example, the items are ordered vertically; in other charts you may choose to order them horizontally. Finally, *additional elements* like text can help convey the main idea, for example, by making it explicit in the title (e.g., "Sales are decreasing in the last quarter") or adding additional information. In our examples, the ranking position of the company has been added for each attribute. Other additional elements are pointers and frames (as you can see in the graphs in figure 76).

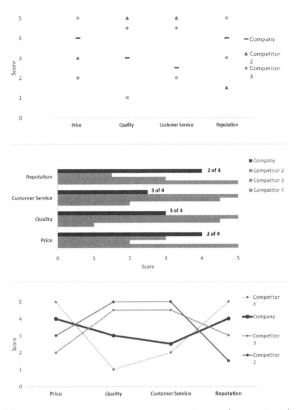

Figure 75: How to use contrast to communicate the main idea (Source: Adapted from Cole Nussbaumer Knaflic, Storytelling With Data)

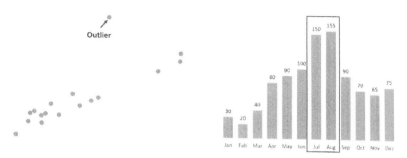

Figure 76: The use of text and markers to convey the main idea
(Source: Adapted from Scott Berinato, Good Charts)

In the following examples, a train company analyzes the reasons for not choosing the train versus other means of transportation. The importance of each element is not only shown by its popularity, but also by whether the company can do something about it. For this reason, the analyst decided that the most important elements are price quality and the absence of Wi-Fi (travel time can't be improved). A light shaded gray is used as the color for less important elements, while a darker shaded gray is used for more important ones, and a more saturated gray is used to highlight the two most important elements (if you can use colors, a possible combination would be shaded gray, shaded blue, blue). The explanatory text uses bold format to further highlight the most important elements, price-quality, and Wi-Fi. If you use blue for price quality and Wi-Fi, the bold text should be blue too. Notice that your attention is unconsciously led to start from the two main elements and then you pass to check the less saturated bars.

235

Reasons for not choosing the train

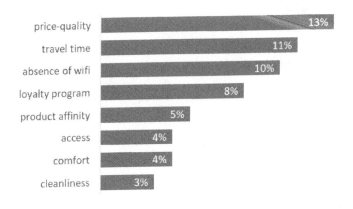

Reasons for not choosing the train

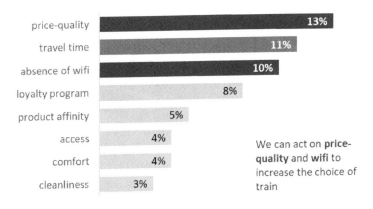

We can act on **price-quality** and **wifi** to increase the choice of train

Figure 77: How to use saturation and text to highlight some information

As you can see, color is quite powerful in creating contrast and driving attention to specific elements. But don't abuse it. Avoid mixing more than four colors; it's preferable if you just use two with different levels of saturation. For instance, you can choose a general shaded gray for "normal" elements and a more saturated blue for the elements that have to stand out. Try to avoid using bright and highly saturated colors since they tire the eye. Instead, use less saturated and natural ones (as explained in the section about design).

The graph in figure 78 has a darker line that stands out from the rest of elements, which are in a shaded gray. In addition, your focus goes toward the right part of the graph where the data points are labeled with values, which is the part where the two lines show a significant gap. In addition, to make it more straightforward, the graph has appropriate axis labels, a title that convey a clear message ("we need you to employ more people"), and additional text has been added to further explain the situation (the gap between tickets received and processed has widened since two employees quit in May).

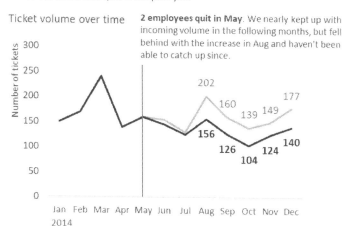

Need to hire 2 FTEs
to backfill those who quit in the past year

Ticket volume over time

2 employees quit in May. We nearly kept up with incoming volume in the following months, but fell behind with the increase in Aug and haven't been able to catch up since.

Figure 78: The use of saturation, labels, and text to convey the main idea (Source: Adapted from Cole Nussbaumer Knaflic, Storytelling With Data)

Another positioning technique is the modification of reference points to emphasize the main idea. For example, you can remove reference points by eliminating some less important details to make your point clearer. In the example in figure 79, age groups have been reduced and attributes have been grouped by age. You will notice that the second chart clearly shows the divide between young and elder people.

WHAT ARE THE MOST IMPORTANT ASPECTS WHEN BUYING THIS PRODUCT

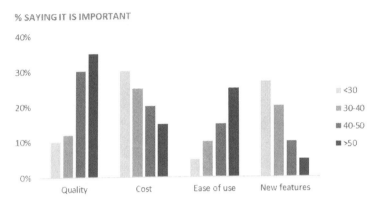

OPPOSING DESIRES OF THE YOUNGS AND OLDS

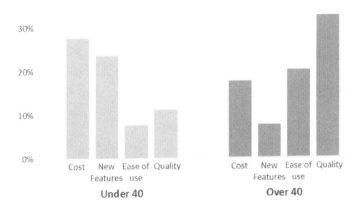

Figure 79: Example of removing reference points

Sometimes, instead of reducing reference points, you need to add some to explain your main idea, for example, when you split a category into subgroups. On some occasions, to make the idea more understandable to the audience, you may shift the reference point by using something more familiar to them. In the graph in figure 80, instead of showing the total amount of hours wasted per year for each task, it shows the days of work lost each year by a worker. Since "days of work" and "workers" are familiar concepts for managers, they can better grasp the amount of time lost. The same concept is used to better explain large numbers, namely when in documentaries you hear that the surface of something is X football fields or certain companies generate so much revenue as the GDP of that country, and so forth.

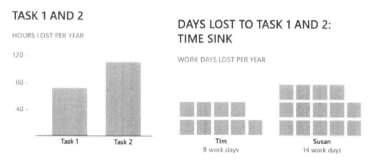

Figure 80: Example of adding reference points (Source: Adapted from Scott Berinato, Good Charts)

Another way you can shift the reference point is by using unit charts instead of shapes (bars, pies, etc.) to represent people, money, or probability. Since unit charts give a sense of individuality, they usually convey the idea better and tend to be more persuasive. In figure 81, the unit chart better represents the idea that only a very small number of high school basketball players make it to the NBA. While the slice in the pie chart is an abstract concept, in the unit chart each point virtually represents a player.

HIGH SCHOOL BASKETBALL PLAYERS TO THE NBA

% OF HIGH SCHOOL BASCKETBALL PLAYERS

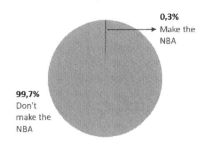

FOR EVERY 10.000 HIGH SCHOOL BASKETBALL PLAYERS, HOW MANY MAKE IT TO THE NBA?

Figure 81: Unit chart as a better alternative compared to a pie chart (Source: Adapted from Scott Berinato, Good Charts)

Sparingly and for well-justified purposes, you can also modify the scale of the axes. As a good practice, axes with values should start at 0 and should have a constant linear scale. However, on some specific occasions, you may opt for a logarithmic scale, namely when there are one or few values that are much larger than the rest or when you want to represent % change or multiplicative factors with absolute numbers. In these cases, with a linear scale, smaller values and variations won't be perceived since their difference is too small compared with the larger values. If you decide to use it, make sure that your audience is used to or can understand it, and clearly say in your graph that you are using a logarithmic scale. Sometimes, however, the problem is not related to variation or outliers; instead, the values you are representing are constantly far from 0. Imagine that you are representing monthly revenues that range from 50 to 55 million and that they vary each month of about 1 million. If you start the vertical axis at 0, changes will look so small they will be barely perceived. In these extreme cases, you may choose to truncate the axis, but remember to make it clear not to mislead your audience. Probably a better solution would be to show in the chart the absolute change or percentage change. You may add somewhere the average monthly revenues if it is important as a reference point for the monthly variations.

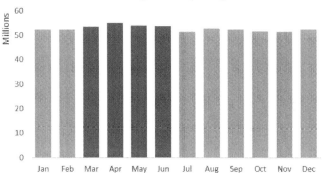

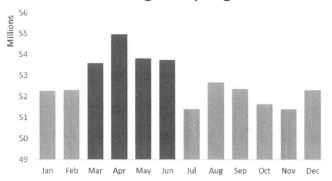

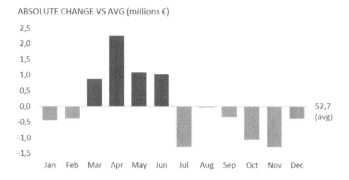

Figure 82: How to deal with scale problems

If truncated axes could be used exceptionally, I don't recommend using double axes. Using double axes is like comparing apple and oranges and the result can be very misleading. An alternative way to compare series with different scales or even different measures is to relativize values (put them in %) in order to adapt them to the same axis and at the same scale.

Box 15: Charts in Presentations

If you include your chart in a digital document sent by email or in a printed version delivered to your audience, you must add as much detail as necessary for them to understand it. Moreover, they will have more time to analyze the graph so they can digest more data and text than they could do during a live presentation. But live presentations present other opportunities; for example, you don't have to include all details since you are there to tell them, they allow you to use animation to better lead your audience toward the main idea, and you can use nonverbal language to support your arguments.

First, when you display a chart in a presentation, wait several seconds before you start talking since your audience is engaged in trying to interpret the visual. If you don't wait, they won't be listening to you carefully and you will disturb their effort to understand the chart. After a few seconds of silence, instead of talking about the chart, talk about the idea, make conclusions, offer hints for further discussion. This, of course, means that the chart is clear enough to be understood without any help. However, in case you present complex charts or the audience is not used to this kind of chart or the topic, you will need to briefly explain how to read the visual. Make sure you show all the information to make conclusions and make your point. In the graphs in figure 83, the comparison of Tom's sales with the desired scores and average scores allow the presenter to make a point on where to invest in training. These graphs probably need a brief introduction, for example, "these are the main characteristics for evaluating sales score."

Figure 83: Comparison of charts to make a point in a presentation
(Source: Adapted from Scott Berinato, Good Charts)

If you have important things to say, you may consider turning off the charts, otherwise, people will be distracted. It can be uncomfortable, so employ it carefully. Or you may just plan to change the slide to a new one with a word concerning this important idea. In the example of spider graphs, you can even show them without labels and comparing different salespeople to make your point. Slides and animation allow you to sequentially overlap these charts to make your point. Even if you only show few elements in the presentation, it does not mean you can't give your audience a more detailed document at the end of it with all the relevant details concerning the graphs (labels, tables with values, etc.). In this document, you can even include other charts that need more time to process the information but that they can reveal additional patterns. The following graph includes extra information that complements the previous ones; you can identify patterns of the sales department as a whole. For instance, you may notice that the sales team is weak in storytelling (it is advisable to use different colors to differentiate salesmen).

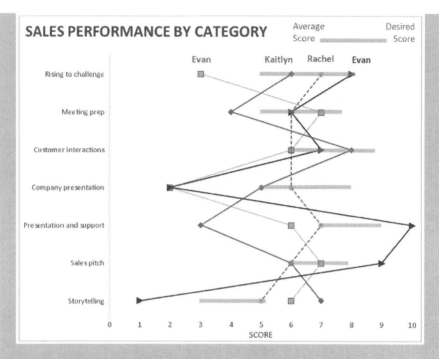

Figure 84: Chart with more details about the sales team
(Source: Adapted from Scott Berinato, Good Charts)

Animation is a useful technique that can be used to better guide your audience. Once you have the final version of your chart, you can deconstruct it and decide to gradually show the different parts in the order you want. Moreover, to reduce the attention toward the first presented elements, when you add a new part, you can de-emphasize the previous ones by removing labels and values or using a less saturated color. For some inspiration, have a look at the videos of fallen.io.

Figure 85: Example of chart suitable for animations in a presentation
(Source: Adapted from Scott Berinato, Good Charts)

REMOVE UNNECESSARY ELEMENTS

Each element must fulfill two requirements to be kept in the visual. First, it must be useful to communicate your idea, or, put another way, without this element you can't communicate your idea, or it will be less clear. Second, if other elements play the same role, it must be the most effective. If this element is necessary and the most effective, ask yourself if you can further improve it by making it more effective or simplifying it.

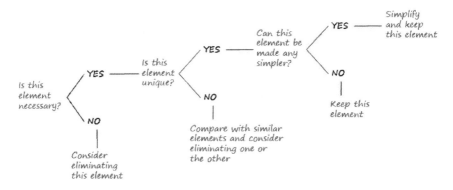

Figure 86: How to choose which elements to keep or eliminate in a chart (Source: Adapted from Scott Berinato, Good Charts)

This approach can be used to decide whether or not to keep each element of your chart, but to speed up the task I've decided to share some practical recommendations:

- Remove borders: According to the proximity and closure principles,[107] you don't need them to separate the chart from the rest, so take them away to lighten up your chart.

---

107 According to the Gestalt principle of proximity, things that are close together appear to be related and part of a whole. The closure principle says that an image doesn't have to be complete to recognize it, since our brain automatically recreates the missing parts. For more information, search for "Gestalt principles" online.

- Remove gridlines to make your important elements stand out (if they are important elements since you don't use data labels and the audience needs to have an idea of values, use a light gray).
- Remove data markers in line graphs if they don't add any additional information.
- Clean up axis labels: The text must be horizontal, names must have an appropriate length (you may use abbreviations), and numbers must have the appropriate level of detail (don't use decimals if the scale is about units, tens, hundreds, etc.); axes titles can be removed if they are obvious (such as dates or years on the horizontal axes).
- Keep axes demarcations at minimum or remove the whole axis if not necessary (it would be redundant if you show data labels).
- Legend: You can label series or categories directly in the chart field instead of creating a legend below it.
- Don't add 3D to graphs; it doesn't add any information and it makes the visualization more difficult to read and misleading.
- Don't repeat axes labels in titles or subtitles; instead, exploit them for showing the question or the answer associated with your visual ("Sales are dangerously decreasing" or "We need to hire more people").
- Push to the background all the secondary elements, important for the message, but that don't have to stand out; you can achieve this by reducing their size and/or using less saturated colors (i.e., light gray).

Finally, the decision to keep or remove each element depends on the audience and on the media you are using. In a printed document, keep more details in case the reader wants to further investigate the issue (e.g., include all data labels), but in a presentation you should be more selective (e.g., include only the essential data labels to make your point).

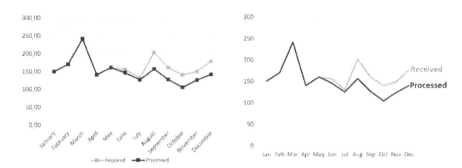

Figure 87: Example of how to create a better chart by removing unnecessary elements (Source: Adapted from Cole Nussbaumer Knaflic, Storytelling With Data)

MAKE IT EASIER FOR YOUR AUDIENCE

In the example in figure 88, the graph has been *simplified* and improved as you can see in the second one. First, having a legend with five colors implies an extra effort for your audience, which you can reduce by using a common x-axis with the different years. Second, you can pass from twenty-five bars to four lines where it is easier to highlight what the graph was meant to highlight: the number of marriages for those who have a bachelor's degree or more. Finally, the decimal points have been removed. They didn't convey any useful additional information.

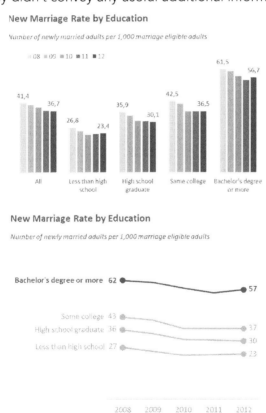

Figure 88: How to simplify a chart by reducing the number of colors, elements, and decimals (Source: Adapted from Cole Nussbaumer Knaflic, Storytelling With Data)

Besides simplification, try to be *consistent*. If you start your presentation with some color pattern, stick to it, otherwise, the audience may be misled. In addition, if you identify a category with a specific color, maintain it throughout the presentation (e.g., the color used to identify a specific competitor). Remember that due to the limits of our short-term memory, we can only keep in mind three to nine visuals; so the more colors (or other elements) you use, the more effort is needed. The only elements that can sometimes exceed this limit are bars and lines, which we can easily compare. Another limit is the number of tonalities of a color we can distinguish. In general, if you are using gray for secondary data in a graph, you can use up to five shades of gray.

Limit the number of colors ideally to two (two hues, for example, blue and gray). To achieve this, you can both reduce the number of categories and, if you finally have more than two categories, use different tonalities of the two colors. In the chart in figure 89, the number of categories is reduced in order to limit the number of tonalities of gray. You could also use two hues to differentiate morning and afternoon sales. For example, 12–6 am in a light yellow, 6 am–12 pm in a darker yellow, 12–6 pm in dark blue, and 6 pm–12 am in light blue.

WHEN DO PEOPLE BUY ON OUR WEBSITE?

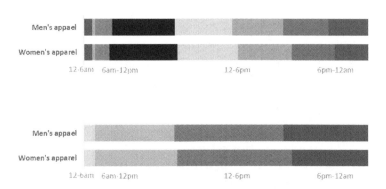

Figure 89: Example of creating categories to simplify the chart
(Source: Adapted from Scott Berinato, Good Charts)

Respect conventions. We are used to seeing time on the horizontal axis, and that it increases from left to right. Good performance goes up and not down, so the y-axis should have values that increase from bottom to top. These expectations are shortcuts that make the processing of information faster. If you don't respect them, first your audience could be misled, and second, they will have to spend time to interiorize the unusual setting. Besides, they could also feel cheated. Other common conventions are:

- Red is bad, green is good
- Blue means colder
- Similar colors = similar items/categories
- Higher saturation = higher value
- Categories are ordered

In the first chart, categories are not ordered, opposite categories have the same color in different tonalities (different color is represented by the pattern), and the pie chart makes it difficult to compare them. On the contrary, the second chart is much easier to understand. Instead of a scale of grays, imagine the second chart with two different colors (hues) that identify interest vs. non-interest. Inside each category, the strongest attitude has a more intense tonality.

HOW INTERESTED ARE YOU IN THIS PRODUCT?

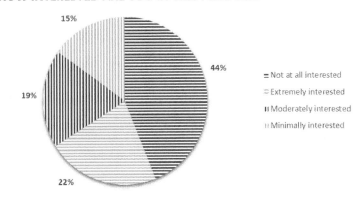

HOW INTERESTED ARE YOU IN THIS PRODUCT?

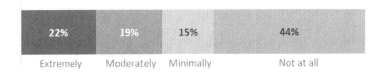

Figure 90: Order and color have been modified to respect
conventions (Source: Adapted from Scott Berinato, Good Charts)

Finally, good charts *limit eye travel* by keeping elements that need
to be looked together in proximate positions, for example, the name of a
series and the depicted line (see Figure 87).

Charts

The best visual to use is the one that can most effectively transmit your message to the audience or the one the audience can read more easily. Often a simple visual is better than a sophisticated one. Therefore, you can do a pretty good job just by using only a handful of visuals properly.[108] The following part of this section will focus on these basic and simple visuals and how to use them properly.

SIMPLE TEXT

When you just have one or two numbers to present, you don't need to use a graph or a table. Just use prominent, simple text. You can also include a brief explanation where you include a second number or specify additional information. In the following example, the solution on the right is better if you want to highlight 20% as a low percentage per se, while the comparison is just additional information that you include in the description.

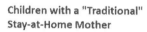

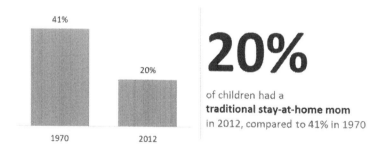

Figure 91: Example of how a simple text can be better than a chart when you want to communicate a specific figure (Source: Adapted from Cole Nussbaumer Knaflic, Storytelling With Data)

---

108 Knaflic, *Storytelling With Data.*

TABLES

Tables are useful when you want your audience to read through it, where each person will go to the columns or rows of interest. Tables are useful to show several individual values over time and categories; however, keep in mind that during a live presentation it may distract your audience who will most probably start reading the table. If you decide to use a table, try to give more prominence to the content and less to the design, for example by using light borders or just white spaces to separate numbers or categories. In the example in figure 92, you have just three lines that separate headers, categories in the first column, and totals. You may also decide to use a line only for totals and headers. Alignment is also quite important. As a rule of thumb, use right alignment for categories in the first column and numbers. With this alignment, each category is more easily related to the rest of the row and numbers are easier to compare to each other in the same column (you have in the same position decimals, ones, tens, etc.).

	Metric1	Metric2	Metric3
Group1	13%	982 €	540 €
Group2	79%	944 €	696 €
Group3	94%	276 €	56 €
Group4	9%	83 €	923 €
Group5	66%	220 €	811 €
Total	**36%**	**2.506 €**	**3.026 €**

Figure 92: Example of table

You can also include visual information in the table by transforming it into a heatmap where the color saturation represents number sizes. This helps the reader to quickly identify lower and higher figures, as well as to surf the table more easily without having to read all the figures. Remember to use a legend "high-low" when you use heatmaps.

	Metric1	Metric2	Metric3
Group1	13%	98%	83%
Group2	79%	54%	96%
Group3	94%	78%	89%
Group4	9%	10%	35%
Group5	66%	50%	82%

Figure 93: Example of heatmap

SCATTERPLOTS

Scatterplots are useful to show the relationship between two variables. For example, you can visualize the relationship between demand and price. You can also exploit color (and sometimes size) to include additional information about the cases (dots) or to include additional variables (this is usually called bubble chart). However, be aware that the more variables you add, the more difficult the interpretation will be. If your audience is not used to such kind of graphs, don't use color and size for additional variables, but use color to help convey the message. In figure 94, the dots with above-average prices are highlighted and an average dotted line is included in the graph.

If the message you want to transmit is about demonstrating a certain correlation, it may be useful to include trend lines (as a rule of thumb, no more than two lines in the same chart).

Cost per mile by miles driven

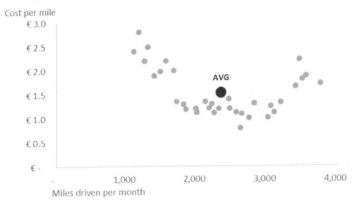

Cost per mile by miles driven

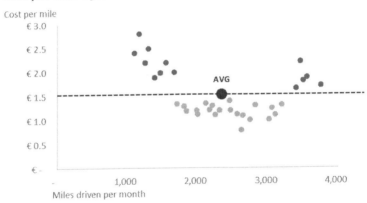

Figure 94: Example of scatterplot (Source: Adapted from Cole Nussbaumer Knaflic, Storytelling With Data)

Scatterplots can also be used to identify distribution. In *Good Charts*, there is an interesting example that analyzes the relationship between travel stress and travel frequency using a scatterplot. The chart shows that there is no correlation, but that travel stress mostly depends on the person (with low frequency different people suffer different levels of stress), probably depending on the character and personal situations. However, it seems that the more they travel, the more they get used to it and the level of stress is quite constant among people.

WHO SUFFERS MOST FROM TRAVEL STRESS?

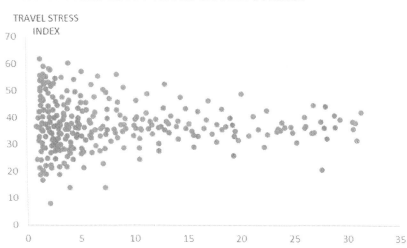

Figure 95: Example of scatterplot used to identify distribution
(Source: Adapted from Scott Berinato, Good Charts)

LINE GRAPHS

They are suitable for representing continuous data on the x-axis often organized in some unit of time such as days, weeks, months, or years. When you want to represent categorical data (e.g., sales by business unit), you should avoid line graphs since the line between data points implies some sort of connection, which you don't have with categorical data. You may also opt for bar charts when you have units of time, but you want to put the focus on individual values. Up to four series can be represented in the same chart; more than that may be difficult to read. Remember to be consistent with the time intervals, namely you should keep the same unit throughout the horizontal axis. Don't switch from decades to years or years to months, since the space between them is always the same and it can be misleading. If the value you are representing is an average or an estimate, you might represent the range or the confidence interval plotting a shaded area around the line.

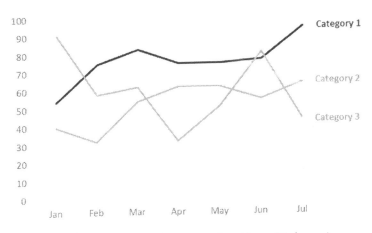

Figure 96: Example of line graph with multiple series

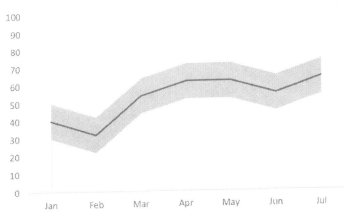

Figure 97: Example of line graph with confidence intervals

Even if it is better to use a zero baseline, you may use a higher value if data fluctuations are small and you want to emphasize them. Just remember to clearly highlight that your y-axis doesn't start at zero. In the example in figure 98, color and thickness are used to highlight important elements, lines are directly labeled, and axes are labeled (the original chart has the two lines in color blue while the rest of the chart is in light gray).

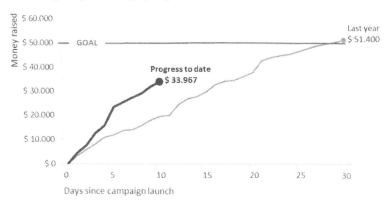

Annual giving campaign progress

Figure 98: Example of line graph with additional elements (Source: Adapted from Cole Nussbaumer Knaflic, Storytelling With Data)

In the example in figure 99, the part concerning the forecast is clearly differentiated using a dotted line and different data markers. In this case, the use of a dotted line serves a specific purpose, but in other situations, it is usually better to represent different series with solid lines. In the solid line, data markers are only present for the described events, while for the forecast they are all present. Notice also the different format of data markers that makes them stand out more.

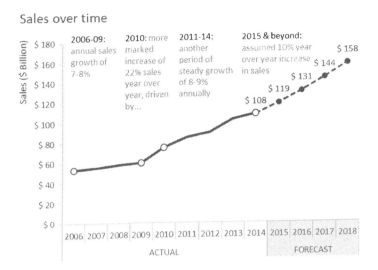

Figure 99: Example of line graph with forecast data and described events (Source: Adapted from Cole Nussbaumer Knaflic, Storytelling With Data)

SLOPEGRAPHS

They are useful when you compare two values, usually when you represent the variation from one time period to another. For example, when you are comparing the satisfaction of different items in a survey and you want to highlight the variation of this year versus last year. Besides the actual values, the plotted line visually shows you the change in direction (increase or decrease) and the size of the variation (depending on the slope). Be careful not to use this graph when too many lines are overlapping. To improve the visualization, you can highlight one or more lines that are important for communicating the main idea. In the example in figure 100, a category has been highlighted over the rest to communicate the alarming decrease in clients' satisfaction about the price.

Clients' satisfaction over time

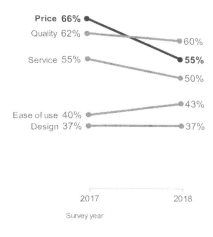

Figure 100: Example of slopegraph[109]

BARS

Bar charts are easy to read for your audience since their eyes almost naturally will compare the endpoints of the bars and will identify proportions and differences. They should be preferred to line charts when you need to show values by nominal or ordinal categories. Due to this specific way of reading them, bar charts should have a zero baseline; otherwise, people may be misled by the visualization. Moreover, for better aesthetics, space between bars should have an adequate size, say half of the column width.

---

109 For this chart I have to thank Cole Nussbaumer Knaflic for the template that you can find at www.storytellingwithdata.com/slopegraph-template.

Figure 101: Example of the biases produced with a non-zero baseline

For bar charts, and for all kinds of graphs in general, try to reduce the clutter to a minimum. It is a good practice to put the y-axis with labels on the left or eliminate it if you are using data labels. This choice depends on the level of detail you want to show. As you may have noticed, in the previous example, y-axes have not been removed even if we should, but it was done with the purpose of showing the change in the starting point.

You can also use several series of data but don't abuse them (the more you add, the more it will be difficult to read). Categories and series (if you have more than one series in each category) should be sorted either logically (e.g., ascending order for age groups) or by their value (depending on where you what to put the attention). Exploit order to convey additional meaning with your graphs.

An alternative to bar charts is stacked bar charts when you want to represent not only the total but also subcategories or the composition of each category. However, with these graphs, it is difficult to compare the subcategories beyond the bottom one. If the comparison between all the categories is important you should opt for presenting the information using more than one chart with different points of view (see figure 102).

Sales by channel (2015-2018)

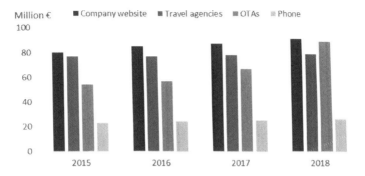

Sales by channel (2015-2018)

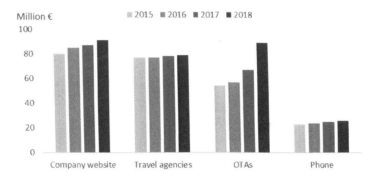

Sales by channel (2015-2018)

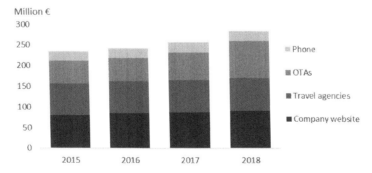

Figure 102: Different ways to represent the same information with bar charts

Stacked bar charts can also be used to represent positive and negative values of the same category. In figure 103, revenues and expenses are represented with bars above and below the x-axis, while profits are represented with a superposed bold line (which is the sum of the other two categories).

Profits are slowly declining

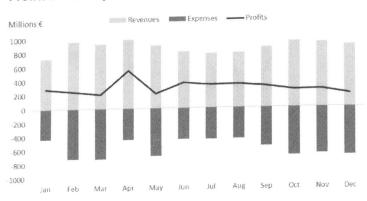

Figure 103: Example of combined bar and line chart

The comparison of compositions is easier using a 100% bar chart (a chart whose bars sum to 100%), but in this case, you lose the visual difference among the totals. If you use 100% stacked bar charts, it may be useful to also include absolute numbers to give your audience an idea of the absolute size of each category.

I prefer horizontal bar charts instead of vertical ones when category labels are too long (and it is difficult to read them in a vertical bar chart) or when the number of categories is large. Since we read from left to right and from top to bottom (following a sort of "z" with our eyes), in a horizontal bar chart you first read the category label and then you see the bar. Before visualizing the size and numbers, you already know the category, and this facilitates the reading of the graph.

Sometimes it may be useful to show two different variables in the same graph, for example, revenues and number of clients. Since these two variables don't have the same scale and measurement unit, people usually add a secondary y-axis. However, this solution makes the audience compare the two variables in a biased way. Instead of adding a second y-axis, create two separate graphs one above the other with the same x-axis (figure 104). Alternatively, use two y-axes, hide them, and directly label data.

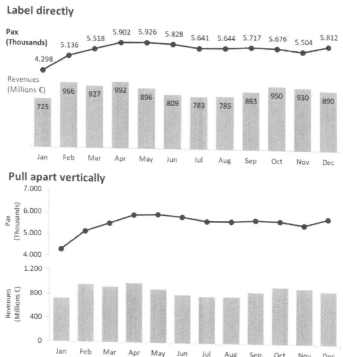

Figure 104: Two alternatives of how to put
different variables in the same chart

In the 100% stacked bar chart in figure 105, titles and labels are properly aligned and positioned. Several elements lead the attention toward the increase in the number of projects that missed goals: dark gray color (originally in red), data labels, and right-aligned text above the graph. In addition, the category of missed goals starts from the bottom line, which makes it easier to compare the evolution.

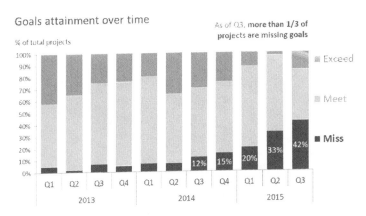

Figure 105: Example of 100% stacked column chart (Source: Adapted from Cole Nussbaumer Knaflic, Storytelling With Data)

Notice the position used in the following graph to give the idea of today's directors decreasing number (bottom line category) with a semi-transparent gray on the negative part of the graph to show that the number of directors leaving is increasing while those that stay are decreasing. On the positive part, we have directors coming from acquisitions and promotions, and the unmet need (highlighted with text and data labels). A footnote explaining how the forecast has been made would be useful.

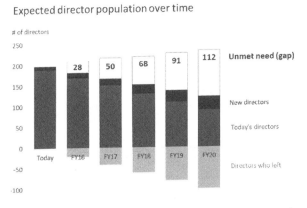

Figure 106: Example of column chart with positive and negative values to highlight the evolution of two categories (Source: Adapted from Cole Nussbaumer Knaflic, Storytelling With Data)

Satisfaction is stronger for price

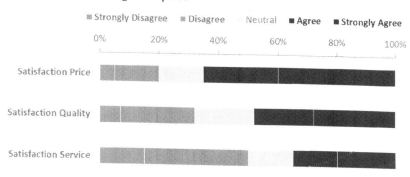

Figure 107: Example of horizontal 100% stacked bar chart used for a satisfaction survey (Source: Adapted from Cole Nussbaumer Knaflic, Storytelling With Data)

In the example in figure 108, despite the great amount of information, color and order have been used to emphasize the three main priorities (in the original chart, the first three priorities were in blue contrasting with the gray of the rest). The horizontal stacked bar chart is useful here on one side because it allows to make the three priorities to stand out clearly, and, on the other side, to better read category labels. Notice that percentage values are maintained (in this case, we assume it is important to give this detail) and they are aligned on the left to make them less "messy."

Top development priorities

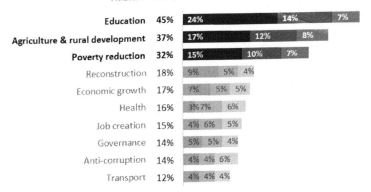

Figure 108: Example of horizontal stacked bar chart with several categories (Source: Adapted from Cole Nussbaumer Knaflic, Storytelling With Data)

A special example of column chart is the "waterfall chart." These charts are suitable for representing a starting point and how we reach an ending point through increases and decreases. An example would be if you have to present the deviation from this year's sales objective through the impact of several factors. Your starting point is the objective, your endpoint is actual sales, and the factors that impacted the results are the middle increases and decreases (e.g., a new competitor entered the market, a problem with the distribution, etc.).

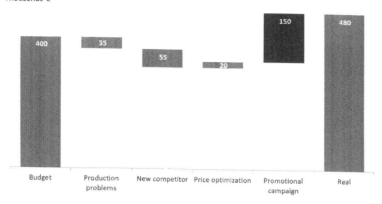

Figure 109: Example of waterfall chart

PIE CHARTS

Try to avoid pie charts whenever possible. The human mind is not very good at comparing different areas, but it is quite good at comparing one-dimension bars. The only case where we can successfully compare areas in a pie chart is when we deal with quarters or halves. Going from a pie chart to a bar chart you may lose the idea of all categories being part of a whole, but the audience will better perceive the differences among categories. In case you consider using a pie chart necessary, don't use more than five categories (if you have more, group them in "other" category) and order slices properly. However, don't use two pie charts to contrast the composition of two elements; instead, use a 100% staked bar chart with two columns.

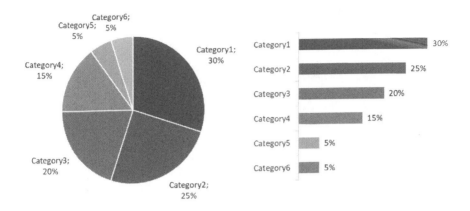

Figure 110: Difference between a pie chart and
a bar chart for "part-of-a-whole" data

OTHER CHARTS

With the abovementioned charts, it will be enough for the great majority of results you may ever have to present. However, in some cases, depending on the complexity of the message and on the sills of your audience, you may choose to use some less "user-friendly" graphs. Have a look at the blog "The Data Visualization Catalogue" where you can find quite a few charts and visualization types.[110] Some interesting ones are alluvial diagrams, map charts, network graphs, Marimekko charts, boxplots, and unit charts.

---

110 https://datavizcatalogue.com/index.html

Dashboards

To create a good dashboard, it is not enough to put together a bunch of well-designed graphs. Of course, the same recommendations about design and data visualization are also valid in this case, but the quality of dashboards also depends on their composition, on the interrelations among their parts, and on the chosen metrics. Stephen Few defined a dashboard:

> A dashboard is a visual display of the most important information needed to achieve one or more objectives; consolidated and arranged on a single screen so the information can be monitored at a glance.[111]

Depending on the purpose, dashboards can be grouped into three categories:

- Strategic dashboards: Used mainly by executives, their goal is to inform about the general performance of the company without many details. They usually are quite static.
- Analytical dashboards: They offer more details compared to the strategic ones, and they allow to drill down into the data (to a certain limit) to discover possible causes of a specific performance.
- Operational dashboards: They are more dynamic and more often updated. They provide specific and updated information used to improve operations.

The indicators to be included must be chosen carefully since you can pick a few of them. They usually are represented by a comparison (with another time period, a target, a forecast, some average, another measure, etc.) or an evolution in time. It is beyond the scope of this book to cover the issue of indicators choice, also because it heavily depends on

---

111 Stephen Few, "Dashboard Confusion," *Perceptual Edge* (March 2014).

the characteristics and needs of the business. For this reason, you need to first know the business ("Know the Business"), then define an analytics strategy ("Think Strategically"), and finally, choose the most suitable indicators. I suggest you have a look at the books *Information Dashboard Design* and *The Lean Startup* for this last step (see Bibliography).

In the rest of this chapter, I will focus on design, mainly inspired by Stephen Few.[112] I want to start with the main mistakes he identified in dashboard design:

- Exceeding single page: Either by scrolling down or by making users change pages, dashboards lose their "at a glance" communicating power. Due to the limits of our short-term memory, we need to see at a glance all the information, or else it will be like reading a report with several pages.
- Inadequate context for the data: When you present a number, a ratio, an evolution, etc., you must provide some context to make users understand how to interpret it. The context may be the same ratio last month, or the average ratio of the industry, or where the target is.
- Excessive detail: For example, showing $1,252,897 instead of $1.2M.
- Deficient measures: Not using the best measure to clearly and efficiently communicate the message. For example, if you show revenues and costs to make a point about profits, you should show directly profits instead.
- Inappropriate display media: Using a graph when a table would have been the best choice.
- Meaningless variety: Visual elements must be chosen based on their effectiveness in conveying a message maintaining a certain consistency.

---

112 Stephen Few, *Information Dashboard Design: The Effective Visual Communication of Data* (Sebastopol, CA: O'Reilly, 2006). The information that follows is mainly based on this book.

- Poorly designed display media: As explained earlier in this book, color should be properly used, as well as size and other visual elements.
- Quantitative data inaccuracy: It means displaying something that is misleading (e.g., a vertical bar chart with the baseline not at zero).
- Data poorly arranged: The positioning and relative size of the visual elements are very important to communicate properly.
- Important data are not highlighted effectively, or not included at all in the dashboard.
- Useless decoration: White spaces are better than decorations.
- Misuse of colors.
- Unattractive visual display: You should make it visually attractive without adding unnecessary distractions.

PRINCIPLES OF DASHBOARD DESIGN

Designing a dashboard is quite a challenge since you have to squeeze a lot of information into a reduced space without losing clarity or leaving out important information. Dashboards must be simple, well-organized, customized to the audience and objectives, and include concise and effective visuals. They have to allow your audience to immediately recognize what deserves attention, but they don't need to display all the details. For this reason, there are four main actions you should undertake to improve their design:

- Eliminate useless non-data elements.
- Reduce the emphasis on useful non-data elements.
- Eliminate unnecessary data elements.
- Emphasize important data elements.

ELIMINATE USELESS NON-DATA ELEMENTS

Non-data elements are those parts of visuals that don't transmit data information, for example, the borders of a graph. Useless non-data elements include:

- Meaningless use of colors (e.g., the use of different colors in a vertical bar chart where series are already differentiated by being in a different position in the x-axis)
- Use of borders in graphs or parts of a dashboard when simple blank or white space is enough
- Gradient colors instead of a solid one when the gradient implies no meaning
- Use of gridlines when bars or lines have value labels or when identifying the value is not necessary
- Alternate colors in the rows of a table when white or blank space is enough
- Use of 3D charts
- Use of decorations

REDUCE EMPHASIS ON USEFUL NON-DATA ELEMENTS

Sometimes, non-data elements are useful, so after leaving only the necessary ones, you should try to reduce their emphasis to highlight data-elements. To achieve this, you can:

- Use lighter and less saturated colors, e.g., a light gray.
- Reduce the size of elements, e.g., reduce the line width.
- Make these elements consistent (same color, size, type) to make them less noticeable.

Other necessary elements that should be de-emphasized are command buttons and text instructions. You should make them less intrusive, for example by placing them in less relevant positions (bottom-right corner) and by using light colors. In the case of text instructions, you may put them on a different page that can be reached by a link.

ELIMINATE UNNECESSARY DATA ELEMENTS

This not only implies choosing the main indicators and data, but also reducing unnecessary details. Since a dashboard has to provide a lot of information in a lesser space, information must be concise. After eliminating unnecessary information, use two main methods to reduce details:

- Summarization: Instead of showing the most detailed data, you show just a sum or an average.
- Exceptions: Only display information when something is out of the normal situation, when it represents a possible opportunity or problem.

An interesting way of reducing details is aggregating data in different time frames: daily data for the current month, monthly data for the months to date, and yearly data for the last few years.

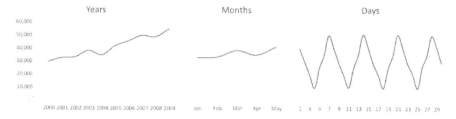

Figure 111: Example of data aggregated in
different time frames to reduce details

EMPHASIZE IMPORTANT DATA ELEMENTS

To emphasize important data elements, start with positioning. Don't waste important dashboard positions with less important information. Have a look at the following example as a guide about the hierarchy you can establish by simply using positioning.

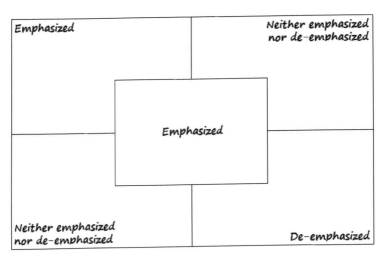

Figure 112: Emphasis by position (Source: Stephen
Few, Information Dashboard Design)

Besides positioning, you can use color, size, and enclosure:

- Color: Use a different color (brighter, darker, or more saturated, for example, the blue color versus the light gray presented in the examples of the previous sections).
- Size: Use bigger graphs or wider lines.
- Enclosure: The "responsible and seldom" use of fill colors or borders.

Finally, remember that the more information you highlight, the less each piece of information will stand out from the rest, so you should carefully decide which elements to highlight.

USING THE BEST VISUALS

This topic was widely covered in the previous section; however, here I will give some more details especially from the point of view of dashboard design. In this part, I will talk not only about graphs, but also about the other useful visual elements of a dashboard: icons, drawing objects, and organizers.

TABLES AND GRAPHS

Tables in dashboards are useful when the importance is on individual values, while when you want to transmit evolution, proportions, or comparison, a graph is more suitable. In this category, I would also include the presentation of a single bold number with its label, which could be considered as a table with just one figure.

	Metric1	Metric2	Metric3
Group1	13%	982 €	540 €
Group2	**79%**	**944 €**	**696 €**
Group3	94%	276 €	56 €
Group4	9%	83 €	923 €
Group5	66%	220 €	811 €
Total	36%	2,506 €	3,026 €

Figure 113: Example of table with important text and figures in bold

Gauges and meters have some important pitfalls. Gauges, due to their circular shape, occupy a lot of space, and, together with meters, the decoration may be distracting. This makes them not the best visual to convey information. Stephen Few proposes a different kind of graph that he calls "bullet graph." It includes the concept of a meter in the simplicity of a bar chart. It is composed of a thin bar that stands out that represents the actual performance measure, on which we can add one or more reference points (e.g., target or last year performance) using a specific shape (e.g., a perpendicular small line). In the background, you can add a bar where the typical red-yellow-green colors give a certain context about how to read the performance. However, instead of using different hues, you can use the same hue with different levels of saturation. You can use this kind of graph both horizontally or vertically (personally I prefer the horizontal one) and you can combine more bullet graphs to compare the performance of different indicators.

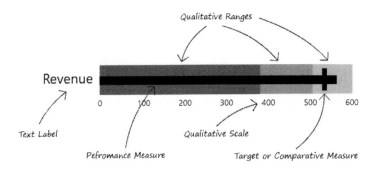

Figure 114: Anatomy of a bullet chart (Source:
Stephen Few, Information Dashboard Design)

Like in bar charts, if you use bars you start the axis at zero, but if the difference with the reference point and the bar is little, and you want to highlight it, you can start with a higher value. In this case, instead of using a bar, you can use just points, for example, a circular shape for the actual performance, and a small vertical line (if you use horizontal bullet graphs) for the reference point.

Figure 115: Bullet chart with a small difference between the target and
the actual value (Source: Stephen Few, Information Dashboard Design)

If you have a future reference point and you want to show the actual performance and the forecasted performance, you can play with a different saturation for the performance bar (see example in figure 116).

Figure 116: Bullet chart with both the actual value
and the forecasted value vs. the target (Source:
Stephen Few, Information Dashboard Design)

A special kind of line chart used in dashboards called Sparkline was proposed by Edward R. Tufte. These are small-size charts with just a single line that shows a specific trend without any other graphic element (axis, scales, text). They may be used with single figures to give more information about the context and they provide more valuable information than a simple up/down arrow. It is recommended to add a small text explaining the time frame.

$ 712,508

Figure 117: Example of Sparkline

ICONS

In dashboards, we may use principally two types of icons: alert icons and up/down icons. Alert icons draw the attention toward some information that deserves it, for example, a dangerous decrease in some indicator performance. Remember, the less you use, the more effective they will be. To create alerts, you can employ different hues (e.g., green, yellow, red) but you may opt instead for one hue with different saturation (more appropriate for colorblind people). In addition, effectiveness increases when icons appear and disappear, instead of always being there.

The up/down icons are used to visually reinforce the positive or negative performance of some indicator. It is recommended to use simple icons (triangles or arrows); you may choose saturation instead of hue to make it more suitable for colorblind people.

DRAWING OBJECTS

Since a dashboard is not just a bunch of isolated graphs on a single page or screen, sometimes drawing objects (lines, arrows, shades, borders) is useful to represent the relationship between the different visualizations. In the following examples, bullet charts are related to lines creating a hierarchy that leads toward the most important indicator, whose performance depends on the performance of the previous ones. In the following example, the indicator "Profit" is the result of the indicators "Revenue" and "Costs."

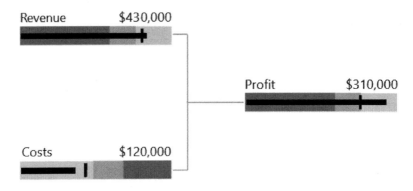

Figure 118: Example of drawing objects used to relate bullet charts

ORGANIZERS

Organizers are visual elements or patterns used to better organize the information and to convey specific meanings. For example, you can organize your data or visuals in tables: organize them into rows or/and columns. Graphs too can be organized either vertically or horizontally when you want to show additional dimensions and it is not feasible to add them in the graph itself. In figure 119, the additional dimension is the "type of travel class," which varies in each graph, while you maintain the two series ("Last Year Pax" and "Current Year Pax") and you use the same y-axis (Travel routes). Another kind of organizer is maps, where you can add qualitative information about the dimension of location. However, you should use spatial maps only when strictly necessary, for example, if you have a lot of locations. With few locations, the information would be better communicated by a simple graph (e.g., a bar chart with different locations on one of the axes).

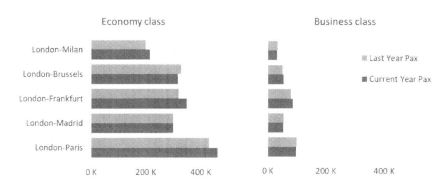

Figure 119: Multiple bar charts as organizers for showing information
with three dimensions (passengers by class, route, and year)

USABILITY

The way you organize different elements, how you preserve the consistency among them, and the overall aesthetics of a dashboard heavily impact its usability.

The organization and grouping of items should be made taking into consideration how the audience will use the information. Some recommendations are:

- Organize groups according to business departments or functions.
- Locate together or nearby elements of the same group.
- Delineate groups using the least visible elements, preferring location and white space over lines, borders, fill colors, etc.
- Promote meaningful comparison by placing related elements in the same table or graph, closer one another, linking them with common visual elements (e.g., color) or using comparative values (ratios, percentages, etc.).

Check your dashboard to eliminate possible meaningless comparisons that may arise by chance; for example, if you use red for negative alerts, you should avoid using it in another graph for a certain series since it may be interpreted as negative.

Since every change we can spot in a dashboard makes us think about the meaning of this change, you must maintain a certain consistency, namely maintaining the same visual characteristics for those elements that transmit the same meaning. For example, you should use the same type of graph to represent sales per month and expenses per month.

If you are creating a dynamic dashboard that allows drilling down and slicing data, make consistent launch actions and make them intuitive. Examples are clicking the bars of a chart to access additional information about that specific category or pop-ups that show the value of data points.

Finally, you should take care of the overall aesthetics of your dashboard because if it is more enjoyable it prepares the audience to get greater insights. Improving aesthetics doesn't mean adding meaningless decoration or adding elements that may reduce usability, but to improve those useful elements from a visual point of view. Some recommendations are:

- Pursue simplicity.
- Choose colors appropriately (except for elements that need attention, use less saturated less bright colors).
- Use a pale background to reduce the stronger contrast using a white background.
- Use high resolution.
- Use an easy-to-read text format (Arial or Verdana among the "sans serif").

IN PRACTICE . . .

When you start designing your dashboard, you should first identify what needs to be communicated and what are the metrics that best represent it. It depends on the specificities of your business and on the audience of your dashboard. This is not a trivial part, but it is so specific that it goes beyond the scope of this book. However, once you have defined that, you have a set of common questions you should ask yourself for each metric:

- Which kind and level of summarization?
- Which unit of measure?
- What complementary information would improve its understanding?
- What are the best means of display?
- What is its relative importance compared to the other metrics?
- In which sequence is the audience expecting to read it?
- To which metric it should be compared with?

A good practice is to meet with the future audience of your dashboard and submit it to other people to test it. In the example provided by Stephen Few (figure 120), you can have a look at some of the best design practices described so far. More saturated colors are only used for data that need to stand out (dark gray bars) while the rest is in less saturated grays. Alerts are used sparingly to effectively draw attention to some metrics. White space is used to create groups of visuals instead of lines or fill color. Space is organized efficiently thanks to sparklines and bullet graphs.

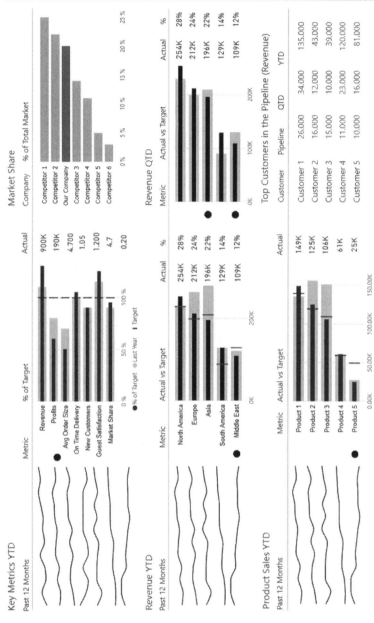

Figure 120: Example of a dashboard (Source: adapted from Stephen Few, Information Dashboard Design)

Conclusion

I hope you enjoyed reading this book as much as I enjoyed writing it. But most importantly, I hope you learned valuable things you can apply right now to be a better analyst. It doesn't matter whether you are an experienced data analyst or a beginner, you can start right away to apply what you've learned: the basics of non-technical skills to succeed in your data analyses.

I know that the information can be overwhelming at the beginning, and that it is difficult to apply all the suggestions explained here. An easy way to start is to apply some of them, and then keep increasing the amount of suggestions you will use. For example, choose a couple of creative techniques, the ones that most inspire you, and use them the next time you face a challenging problem. When you have to analyze something, don't focus only on inferential statistics, but consider also the power of the Bayesian approach, analytics, or heuristics. When you draw your next chart, prepare a checklist of the most important suggestions explained in this book and go through them before showing it: is it the most effective visual? Are there useless or redundant elements? Is it easy to understand?

Imagine yourself presenting your next analysis. Imagine you give a good speech, with a beautiful presentation with such good charts that your audience will be astonished. People are looking at you differently. After the presentation, everybody is congratulating you on the job well done. Now use this feeling to get the strength to keep improving your style and your non-technical skills. You may start by having a look at the books and links in the following Bibliography. Don't be in a hurry. Learning is a lifelong process. And remember, non-technical skills are the most underestimated, but not the less important. Now you have a huge advantage compared to those who don't have them. Exploit it!

Bibliography

http://downloads.soappresentations.com/10_worst_body_language_presentation_mistakes

http://extremepresentation.typepad.com/files/choosing-a-good-chart-09.pdf

http://soappresentations.com/downloads/

http://www.ramonvullings.com/free-downloads/

https://datavizcatalogue.com/

https://www.balancedscorecard.org

https://www.coursera.org/learn/presentation-skills/home/welcome

https://www.edge.org/conversation/nassim_nicholas_taleb-the-fourth-quadrant-a-map-of-the-limits-of-statistics

https://www.forbes.com/sites/valleyvoices/2017/01/31/the-rise-of-ai-will-force-a-new-breed-of-data-scientist/#3a7f08db2539

https://www.kdnuggets.com/2018/11/data-science-activities-business-initiatives-hypothesis-development-canvas.html

https://www.mindtools.com/pages/article/newCT_05.htm

https://www.ted.com/talks/giorgia_lupi_how_we_can_find_ourselves_in_data

https://www.ted.com/talks/hans_rosling_shows_the_best_stats_you_ve_ever_seen

www.beyondbulletpoints.com

www.extremepresentation.com

Anderson, Chris. 2008. "The End of Theory: The Data Deluge Makes the Scientific Method Obsolete." *Wired.*

Anderson, Chris. 2009. *The Long Tail: How Endless Choice Is Creating Unlimited Demand.* New York: Random House Business.

Anderson, Chris. 2010. *Free: How Today's Smartest Businesses Profit by Giving Something for Nothing.* New York: Hyperion.

Ariely, Dan. 2010. *Predictably Irrational: The Hidden Forces That Shape Our Decisions.* New York: Harper Perennial.

Atkinson, Cliff. 2011. *Beyond Bullet Points: Using Microsoft© PowerPoint© to Create Presentations That Inform, Motivate, and Inspire.* Redmond, WA: Microsoft Press.

Beall, Anne E. 2010. *Strategic Market Research: A Guide to Conducting Research That Drives Businesses.* Bloomington, IN: IUniverse.

Berinato, Scott. 2016. *Good Charts: the HBR Guide to Making Smarter, More Persuasive Data Visualizations.* Boston, MA: Harvard Business Review Press.

Bono, Edward De. 1993. *Serious Creativity: Using the Power of Lateral Thinking to Create New Ideas.* New York: HarperCollins Publishers.

Bono, Edward De. 2015. *Lateral Thinking: Creativity Step by Step*. New York: Perennial Library.

Brighton, Henry, and Gerd Gigerenzer. 2012. "Homo Heuristics and the Bias–Variance Dilemma." *Action, Perception and the Brain* 68–91.

Butler-Bowdon, Tom. 2017. *50 Psychology Classics: Your Shortcut to the Most Important Ideas on the Mind, Personality, and Human Nature*. London: Nicholas Brealey.

Carnegie, Dale. 1998. *How to Win Friends and Influence People*. New York: Pocket Books.

Cialdini, Robert B. 1985. *Influence: How and Why People Agree to Things*. Fort Mill, SC: Quill.

Craig, Juana Clark. 2012. *Project Management Lite: Just Enough to Get the Job Done ... Nothing More*. North Charleston, SC: CreateSpace.

Davenport, Thomas H., and Jeanne G. Harris. 2007. *Competing on Analytics: The New Science of Winning*. Boston, MA: Harvard Business School Press.

Duarte, Nancy. 2010. *Resonate: Present Visual Stories That Transform Audiences*. Hoboken, NJ: Wiley.

Ellenberg, Jordan. 2015. *How Not to Be Wrong: The Power of Mathematical Thinking*. New York: Penguin.

Epstein, Robert. 1996. *Creativity Games for Trainers: A Handbook of Group Activities for Jumpstarting Workplace Creativity*. New York: Training McGraw-Hill.

Few, Stephen. 2014. "Dashboard Confusion." *Perceptual Edge*, March 2014.

Few, Stephen. 2006. *Information Dashboard Design: The Effective Visual Communication of Data*. Sebastopol, CA: O'Reilly.

Fisher, Roger, William Ury, and Bruce Patton. 2011. *Getting to Yes*. New York: Penguin.

Gaissmaier, W., and Julian N. Marewski. 2011. "Forecasting Elections with Mere Recognition from Lousy Samples: A Comparison of Collective Recognition, Wisdom of Crowds, and Representative Polls." *Judgment and Decision Making*.

Gardner, Howard. 1999. *Intelligence Reframed: Multiple Intelligences for the 21st Century*. New York: Basic Books.

Gigerenzer, G., and Wolfgang Gaissmaier. 2011. "Heuristic Decision Making." *Annual Review of Psychology*.

Gilovich, Thomas. 1993. *How We Know What Isn't So: Fallibility of Human Reason in Everyday Life*. New York: The Free Press.

Gladwell, Malcolm. 2000. *The Tipping Point: How Little Things Can Make a Big Difference*. Boston, MA: Little Brown.

Gladwell, Malcolm. 2007. *Blink: The Power of Thinking Without Thinking*. New York: Back Bay Books.

Godin, Seth. 1999. *Permission Marketing: Turning Strangers into Friends, and Friends into Customers*. New York: Simon & Schuster.

Godin, Seth. 2001. *Unleashing the Ideavirus: Stop Marketing at People! Turn Your Ideas into Epidemics by Helping Your Customers Do the Marketing for You.* New York: Hachette Books.

Godin, Seth. 2005. *Purple Cow: Transform Your Business by Being Remarkable.* New York: Penguin.

Goldstein, Daniel G., and Gerd Gigerenzer. 2002. "Models of Ecological Rationality: The Recognition Heuristic." *Psychological Review* 109, no. 1: 75–90.

Grant, Adam, and Sheryl Sandberg. 2017. *Originals How Non-Conformists Move the World.* New York: Penguin Publishing Group.

Haq, Rashed. 2014. "Data Analytics: Creating a Roadmap for Success." *CROSSINGS: The Sapient Journal of Trading and Risk Management.*

Henry, Todd. 2013. *The Accidental Creative: How to Be Brilliant at a Moment's Notice.* New York: Penguin.

Kahneman, Daniel. 2012. *Thinking, Fast and Slow.* New York: Penguin.

Kahneman, Daniel, and Gary Klein. 2009. "Conditions for Intuitive Expertise: A Failure to Disagree." *American Psychologist* 64, no. 6: 515–26.

Kaplan, Robert S., and David P. Norton. 2009. *Execution Premium: Linking Strategy to Operations for Competitive Advantage.* Boston, MA: Harvard Business Press.

Kaufman, Josh. 2012. *The Personal MBA: Master the Art of Business.* New York: Portfolio/Penguin.

Kelley, Tom, and David Kelley. 2015. *Creative Confidence: Unleashing the Creative Potential Within Us All*. London: William Collins.

Kelley, Tom, Jonathan Littman, and Thomas J. Peters. 2016. *The Art of Innovation: Lessons in Creativity from IDEO, America's Leading Design Firm*. London: Profile Books.

Kemp, Martin. 2011. *Leonardo*. New York: Oxford University Press.

Kim, W. Chan., and Mauborgne Renée. 2005. *Blue Ocean Strategy: How to Create Uncontested Market Space and Make the Competition Irrelevant*. Boston, MA: Harvard Business School Press.

Knaflic, Cole Nussbaumer. 2015. *Storytelling With Data: A Data Visualization Guide for Business Professionals*. Hoboken, NJ: Wiley.

Kumar, V., J. Andrew Petersen, and Robert P. Leone. 2007. "How Valuable Is Word of Mouth?" *Harvard Business Review*, October 2007.

Lewis, Michael. 2003. *Moneyball: The Art of Winning an Unfair Game*. New York: W. W. Norton.

Lewis, Michael. 2017. *The Undoing Project*. New York: Penguin.

Lindstrom, Martin. 2008. *Buyology: The New Science of Why We Buy*. New York: Doubleday.

Lindstrom, Martin. 2011. *Brandwashed: Tricks Companies Use to Manipulate Our Minds and Persuade Us to Buy*. New York: Crown Business.

Lucas, Stephen E. 2007. *The Art of Public Speaking*. New York: McGraw-Hill.

Madsbjerg, Christian. 2017. *Sensemaking: The Power of the Humanities in the Age of the Algorithm*. New York: Hachette Books.

Madsbjerg, Christian, and Mikkel B. Rasmussen. 2014. "An anthropologist walks into a bar..." *Harvard Business Review*, March 2014.

Madsbjerg, Christian, and Mikkel B. Rasmussen. 2014. *The Moment of Clarity: Using the Human Sciences to Solve Your Hardest Business Problems*. Boston, MA: Harvard Business Review Press.

Marr, Bernard. 2017. *Data Strategy: How to Profit from a World of Big Data, Analytics and the Internet of Things*. London: Kogan Page.

Martin, Roger L. 2009. *The Opposable Mind: Winning Through Integrative Thinking*. Boston, MA: Harvard Business Press.

Mayer-Schönberger Viktor, and Kenneth Cukier. 2013. *Big Data: A Revolution That Will Transform How We Live, Work, and Think*. London: John Murray.

Medow, M. A., and C. R. Lucey. 2011. "A Qualitative Approach to Bayes' Theorem." *Evidence-Based Medicine*, 16, no. 6: 163–67.

Michalko, Michael. 2006. *Thinkertoys: A Handbook of Creative-Thinking Techniques*. New York: Ten Speed Press.

Morgan, Michael. 1993. *Creating Workforce Innovation: Turning Individual Creativity into Organizational Innovation*. Warriewood, NSW, Australia: Business & Professional Pub.

Mousavi, Shabnam, and Gerd Gigerenzer. 2014. "Risk, Uncertainty, and Heuristics." *Journal of Business Research*, 67, no. 8: 1671–78.

Peppers, Don, and Martha Rogers. 2005. *Return on Customer: Creating Maximum Value from Your Scarcest Resource*. New York: Crown Business.

Pillay, Srinivasan S. 2017. "Brain Can Only Take So Much Focus." *Harvard Business Review*, May 2017.

Pillay, Srinivasan S. 2017. *Tinker Dabble Doodle Try: Unlock the Power of the Unfocused Mind*. New York: Ballantine Books.

Pressfield, Steven. 2002. *The War of Art: Winning the Inner Creative Battle*. New York: Rugged Land.

Sawyer, Robert Keith. 2013. *Explaining Creativity: The Science of Human Innovation*. New York: Oxford University Press.

Sawyer, Robert Keith. 2013. *Zig Zag: The Surprising Path to Greater Creativity*. San Francisco, CA: Jossey-Bass.

Scappini, Alberto. 2016. *80 Fundamental Models for Business Analysts: Descriptive, Predictive, and Prescriptive Analytics Models with Ready-to-Use Excel Templates*. Charleston, SC: CreateSpace.

Schutt, Russell K. 2019. *Investigating the Social World: The Process and Practice of Research*. Thousand Oaks, CA: Sage.

Schwartz, Barry. 2004. *The Paradox of Choice Why More Is Less*. New York: HarperCollins.

Silver, Nate. 2012. *The Signal and the Noise: Why So Many Predictions Fail, but Some Don't*. New York: Penguin.

Sober, Elliot. 2012. *Core Questions in Philosophy: A Text with Readings.* 6th ed. Upper Saddle River, NJ: Pearson.

Sterne, Jim. "From Data Scientist to Data Artist." Anametrix (White Paper).

Taleb, Nassim Nicholas. 2005. *Fooled by Randomness: The Hidden Role of Chance in Life and in the Markets.* New York: Random House Trade Paperbacks.

Taleb, Nassim Nicholas. 2010. *The Black Swan: The Impact of the Highly Improbable.* New York: Random House Trade Paperbacks.

Tapscott, Don, and Anthony D. Williams. 2010. *Wikinomics: How Mass Collaboration Changes Everything.* New York: Portfolio.

Tharp, Twyla, and Mark Reiter. 2006. *The Creative Habit: Learn It and Use It for Life: A Practical Guide.* New York: Simon & Schuster.

Tversky, Amos, and Daniel Kahneman. 1974. "Judgment under Uncertainty: Heuristics and Biases." *Science* 185 (September).

Tversky, Amos, and Daniel Kahneman. 1985. "The Framing of Decisions and the Psychology of Choice." *Behavioral Decision Making* 25–41.

Wahl, Erik. 2017. *The Spark and the Grind: Ignite the Power of Disciplined Creativity.* New York: Portfolio/Penguin.

Wheelan, Charles J. 2014. *Naked Statistics: Stripping the Dread from the Data.* New York: W. W. Norton.

Zenko, Micah. 2015. *Red Team: How to Succeed by Thinking Like the Enemy.* New York: Basic Books.

Manufactured by Amazon.ca
Bolton, ON

36808108R00168